Montreat College
School of Adult and Graduate Studies (AGS)

Academic Catalog
2016-2017

Montreat College
2016 – 2017 Academic Catalog

Published by Montreat College, Montreat, NC 28757

This catalog provides general information about Montreat College and summarizes important information about the College's policies, requirements for graduation, regulations, and procedures. It is not intended to establish, nor does it establish, a contractual relationship with students. Rather, the catalog is published to acquaint students with information that will be helpful to them during their college careers.

It is necessary in the general administration of the College to establish requirements and regulations governing the granting of degrees. Academic advisors, department chairs, and academic staff members are available to aid students in understanding these requirements and regulations. It is the student's responsibility, however, to meet them. Students are urged to keep this catalog as a reference.

Changes in curricular requirements may occur during catalog publications. Students will be informed of such changes. When this occurs, students may follow the requirements in effect at the time they entered Montreat College, or they may petition to follow the changed requirements. Students must choose to follow one catalog or the other; they may not pick and choose from the various requirements outlined in two or more catalogs. Reasonable substitutions will be made for discontinued and changed courses.

Information in the catalog is considered to be an accurate representation of Montreat College policy as of the date of publication. The College reserves the right to make such changes in educational and financial policy as the College's Faculty, Administration and/or Board of Trustees may deem consonant with sound academic and fiscal practice. The College has made a good faith effort to avoid typographical errors and other errors in the statements of policy and degree requirements as published. In any case, erroneous catalog statements do not take precedence over properly adopted policies. Please see the College website at www.montreat.edu for the most updated version of the catalog.

Montreat College is an independent, self-governing college, related to the Presbyterian Church by history, location, and long-standing relationships with the Mountain Retreat Association and the Association of Presbyterian Colleges and Universities. The College seeks to honor Jesus Christ and our Presbyterian and Reformed heritage while remaining uninvolved in denominational politics and administration and welcoming students without regard to religious affiliation.

As an institution in the Presbyterian and Reformed tradition, the College seeks to treat all persons equally and emphasizes the dignity and worth of the individual. In compliance with Title IX of the Education Amendments of 1972, Sections 503 and 504 of the Rehabilitation Act of 1973 and the Americans with Disabilities Act, Montreat College admits students of any race, color, religion, sex, age, national or ethnic origin to all rights, privileges, programs, and activities generally accorded or made available to students at the school. It does not discriminate on the basis of race, disability, military service, color, religion, sex, age, national and ethnic origin in administration of its educational policies, admissions policies, scholarship and loan programs, and athletic and other school administrative programs.

In accordance with federal and state statutes, Montreat College is committed to maintaining a community that is free from sexual harassment and all forms of sexual intimidation, exploitation, coercion, and violence. Inquiries concerning the College's policies, compliance with applicable laws, statutes, and complaints may be directed to the Academic Affairs Office, Montreat College, P.O. Box 1267, Montreat, NC 28757, (828) 669-8012 (ext. 3621).

Campus Locations

Montreat College Main Campus
P.O. Box 1267
310 Gaither Circle
Montreat, NC 28757

828-669-8012
800-622-6968
828-669-9554 fax

Black Mountain
Montreat College
191 Vance Avenue
Black Mountain, NC 28711

828-669-8012
800-690-7727
828-669-0500 fax

Charlotte
Montreat College
School of Adult and Graduate Studies
212 South Tryon Street, Ste. 1700
Charlotte, NC 28281

704-357-3390
800-436-2777
704-676-4618 fax

Asheville
Montreat College
School of Adult and Graduate Studies
29 Turtle Creek Drive
Asheville, NC 28803

828-667-5044
800-806-2777
828-667-9079 fax

Morganton
Montreat College
School of Adult and Graduate Studies
PO Box 1389
Morganton, NC 28680-1389

828-475-2431

*Our Online Campus has administrative headquarters at the Montreat, NC location.

Visit us online: www.montreat.edu

Table of Contents

Montreat College

At Montreat College, a student's experience is enhanced by an education of value, grounded in a strong liberal arts core, taught by outstanding Christian faculty, and prized by employers and graduate schools. Students benefit from Montreat College's small classes where their opinions matter and they grow through one-on-one interaction with professors and classmates. Students are challenged to integrate faith and learning while considering subjects in new ways. Hands-on experiences in the majors (internships, field studies, mission programs, community service, and independent research) enable students to gain practical career and life preparation.

Montreat College welcomes students of many denominations and cultural backgrounds, including students from all corners of the world. In a diverse, multicultural environment, students learn how to investigate the unfamiliar, think critically, and communicate and clarify their ideas. In the process, they develop the skills, personal values, and faith to confidently take their place in the world. In the residence halls or over dinner at a professor's house, students find themselves sharing perspectives and exchanging ideas. The distinct spirit of community goes beyond the faculty, staff, and students and extends to visiting Christian conference members, residents of the town of Montreat and neighboring Black Mountain, as well as to the "cottagers" who vacation here throughout the seasons.

Montreat College is a place where students can set themselves apart through an extraordinary range of leadership opportunities on the Montreat Campus. A nationally recognized Discovery Wilderness Program takes advantage of the mountain location and offers a unique twenty-one-day adventure for academic credit. Outdoor recreation opportunities available to students range from hiking to whitewater adventures to snow skiing. Students can also choose from a variety of off-campus volunteer opportunities such as serving at nursing homes, churches, children's homes, and shelters.

Montreat College is a member of the Appalachian Athletic Conference (AAC) of the National Association of Intercollegiate Athletics (NAIA). At Montreat College, men compete in baseball, basketball, cross country, golf, track and field, lacrosse, tennis, and soccer. Women compete in basketball, cross country, golf, track and field, soccer, softball, lacrosse, tennis, and volleyball. Students also enjoy an active intramural program where exciting competition takes place throughout the year.

Montreat College includes the main campus in Montreat and sites in Black Mountain, Asheville, Morganton, and Charlotte. The School of Adult and Graduate Studies seeks to provide adult students a Christ-centered education through evening classes and online.

The School of Adult and Graduate Studies is designed especially for the adult learner who has completed some college work and desires to finish a degree in an accelerated program by attending class one night per week. Through this School, the College offers Associate in Science (AS), Bachelor of Business Administration (BBA), Bachelor of Science in Management (BS), Bachelor of Science in Psychology and Human Services (BS), Bachelor of Science in Bible and Religion (BS), Master of Business Administration (MBA), Master of Science in Environmental Education (MS), Master of Arts in Clinical Mental Health Counseling (MA), and Master of Science in Management and Leadership (MS) degrees.

History

The beauty and tranquility of the Blue Ridge Mountains led Congregationalist minister John C. Collins to form the Mountain Retreat Association in 1897 "for the encouragement of Christian work and living through Christian convention, public worship, missionary work, schools, and libraries." By 1907, J. R. Howerton of Charlotte, NC, conceived and carried out the idea of purchasing Montreat for the Presbyterian Church in the United States. Then, in 1913, Dr. Robert C. Anderson, president of the Mountain Retreat Association, proposed that the grounds and facilities of the Association be used for a school during the academic year. In 1915, the General Assembly decreed "that the property of the Mountain Retreat Association be used for a Normal School and that the establishment of the school be referred to the Synods".

The Synods of Appalachia, Georgia, Alabama, North Carolina, Tennessee, and Virginia elected trustees who met in Montreat on May 2, 1916, and elected Dr. Robert F. Campbell of Asheville, NC, chairman, Mr. W. T. Thompson Jr. of Knoxville, TN, secretary, and Ruling Elder T. S. Morrison of Asheville, NC, treasurer. The Montreat Normal School, a four-year preparatory and two-year college combination, opened its first session in October 1916 with eight students. Montreat Normal School continued to grow over the years. Throughout times of war, economic fluctuations, and rapid social change, the school sought to provide a Christian setting in which to prepare young women to become teachers.

In 1934, during Dr. Robert C. Anderson's tenure as president, Montreat Normal School (College Department) was renamed Montreat College. The College grew as its academic program expanded. It began a four-year degree program in 1945. After 14 years as a four-year women's college, the College was restructured in 1959 as a coeducational junior college and was given a new name, Montreat-Anderson College.

In 1986, the College Board of Trustees, realizing the demands and changing circumstances in higher education, made the decision to become again a baccalaureate institution. The dream of its first president, Dr. Anderson, was for the College to serve as an accredited baccalaureate institution. The College has realized that dream. It returned to the original name of Montreat College in August of 1995, sharing the original vision and identity. The change reflects the Montreat College of today, a four-year college with several growing campuses and a graduate program.

Montreat College's School of Adult and Graduate Studies began as the School of Professional and Adult Studies offering classes on September 19, 1994. The College's Charlotte campus was officially opened on September 11, 1995, and the Asheville campus held its grand opening on October 8, 1996. Montreat College purchased 72 acres of land with 21 buildings in Black Mountain in the summer of 2001, resulting in a total of four Montreat College campuses.

In June 1998, Montreat College was accredited by the Commission on Colleges of the Southern Association of Colleges and Schools as a level three institution to offer the master's degree in business administration. Since then Montreat College has added three more master's degrees to its program offerings: the Master of Science in Management and Leadership, the Master of Science in Environmental Education, and the Master of Arts in Clinical Mental Health Counseling. In January 2013, the College launched its first three fully online degree programs offering its Christ-centered education in the virtual world.

The Presidents of the College have been Dr. Robert Campbell Anderson, 1916–1947; Dr. J. Rupert McGregor, 1947–1957; Dr. Calvin Grier Davis, 1959–1972; Dr. Silas M. Vaughn, 1972–1991; Mr. William W. Hurt, 1991–2002; Dr. John S. Lindberg, 2002–2003; Dr. Dan Struble, 2004–2013; and Dr. Paul J. Maurer, 2014 to the present.

VISION

Montreat College seeks to be a leader in Christ-centered higher education regionally, nationally, and globally.

MISSION

Montreat College is an independent, Christ-centered, liberal arts institution that educates students through intellectual inquiry, spiritual formation, and preparation for calling and career, all to impact the world for Jesus Christ.

STATEMENT OF FAITH

Preamble

The trustees and employees of Montreat College constitute an academic community of caring believers committed to the Lordship of Jesus Christ. Students are welcomed to this Christian community regardless of belief.

Statement of Faith

The trustees and employees commit themselves to the following faith statement drawn from the college's Reformed tradition:

1. We believe in one sovereign God, eternally existing in three persons: God the Father; His only begotten Son, Jesus Christ, our Lord and Savior; and the Holy Spirit, the giver of life. (Daniel 4:25, 35; Mark 12:29; John 1:1, 14, 18; 14:28; 15:26; 16:28; Romans 9:15-23; Revelation 4:11)

2. We believe the Bible, the sixty-six books of the Old and New Testaments, is the infallible Word of God, completely inspired and authoritative, and is to govern Christians in every aspect of life and conduct. (I Thessalonians 2:13; II Timothy 3:16; II Peter 1:21)

3. We believe Jesus is the Christ, the Son of the living God, whom the Father sent into the world to atone for the sin of humanity. Jesus was conceived by the Holy Spirit, born of the Virgin Mary, and lived a life without sin. He was crucified and rose victoriously from the dead. Through His gift of grace, we as believers are redeemed for all eternity and are reconciled to the Heavenly Father. (Luke 1:26-37; 2:6, 7; John 3:16; Romans 3:10, 23; Romans 5:12-15; I John 3:8)

4. We believe the Holy Spirit is a free gift to believers from the Father and the Son to live within us and to empower us to love and obey the Lord and His Word. (John 14:15-17; John 16:5-15; Ephesians 1:13-14)

5. We believe the Triune God is the sole Creator and Sustainer of the universe. God created all things and declared all He created to be good. After creating Adam and Eve in His own image, in a state of original righteousness, and distinct from all other living creatures, the Lord gave to all humanity the responsibility of caring for His world. (Genesis 1-2; John 1:1-18)

6. We believe God's good and perfect creation became tainted in every aspect by sin from humanity's rebellion against God. We acknowledge the existence, evil power, and influence of Satan. (Genesis 3; Ephesians 6:12)

7. We believe the Church is all who believe in and confess Jesus Christ as Savior and Lord and receive God's grace. We are called by God to be His one body of believers, gathered in communities. Empowered by the Holy Spirit, the Church's call is to declare His Good News of salvation to the fallen and lost world, to make disciples, and to serve all who are wounded, broken, and neglected. (Matthew 28:16-20; Mark 16:15-18; Romans 10:9-10; II Corinthians 5:17-21; Ephesians 2:8-9; 4)

8. We believe all those who profess Jesus as Savior and Lord are to follow in His Way and are to live as those who magnify and glorify Him, the Head of His Church. As forgiven followers, we are called to live holy and blameless lives through the power of the Holy Spirit until that time when Jesus Christ shall return in all His glory. (I Corinthians 1:2; Ephesians 4:22-24; Hebrews 10:14; I John 3:4-9; 4:4; 5:1-5)

Adopted by Board of Trustees May 5, 2016

Foundations

We believe humanity is God's creation in His own image, and therefore persons are thinking, relational, moral, and spiritual beings of dignity and worth. We seek to serve students in all these dimensions. Our aim is to challenge students to become the complete person a loving God intends them to be, and to live in vital relationship with Him. Therefore, we seek to be a faith community as well as an academic community. We see our educational mission as an extension of the great ends of the church. We seek to graduate students who are committed to Christian servant-leadership in the world, promoting personal and social righteousness by God's grace and to His glory.

As a Christian College in the Presbyterian tradition, we are guided in our pursuit of academic excellence by the framework of Reformed beliefs. We confess the living God as the ultimate foundation of our faith and the source of all truth. We believe God is revealed perfectly in Jesus Christ. We affirm our Lord and Savior Jesus Christ as the center of history, restoring purpose, order, and value to the whole of life. We believe Jesus Christ to be the focus and culmination of scripture and that God's written Word is inspired, authoritative, and rightly interpreted by the Holy Spirit, our infallible rule for faith, conduct, and worship. We study and address a world and humanity that were created good, corrupted by the fall, redeemed through faith in Christ, and are moving toward the final consummation of God's purposes through the work of the Holy Spirit.

Educational Objectives

Approaching the integration of faith and learning from an informed, biblical perspective, faculty, staff, and students form a Christian community of learners that seeks to pursue the premise that all truth is God's truth and explore the significance of this in the various academic disciplines. We are committed to a thorough exploration of the complementary relationship between biblical truth and academic inquiry. We openly embrace students of all cultures, races, and faiths in an atmosphere of academic excellence, intellectual inquiry, and Christian love.

The College seeks to provide a broad, rigorous liberal arts curriculum with an emphasis on traditional and selected professional degree programs, including degree programs for adult learners. The educational goals of the College are that students will develop the following:

- An informed, biblical worldview that includes the following:
  - The sovereignty of God over all creation and knowledge.
  - A lifestyle of Christian service to others and the community.
  - The recognition of the intrinsic worth of self and all persons.
  - A genuine critical openness to the ideas and beliefs of others.
  - The formation of values and ethical reasoning.
  - An appreciation for what is beautiful, true, and good in the arts and literature.
  - A respect for and attitude of stewardship toward the whole of creation.
  - An understanding of the past and its interconnectedness with the present and future.
- Effective written and oral communication skills.
- Critical thinking and problem-solving skills.
- Essential computer information systems skills.
- Competency in their academic majors.
- Interpersonal and team skills and an understanding and appreciation of their personal strengths and weaknesses.
- Dispositions toward reflective and responsible citizenship needed to fulfill callings as effective leaders and committed laity.

Accreditation

Montreat College is accredited by the Commission on Colleges of the Southern Association of Colleges and Schools to award the associate, bachelor, and master degrees. Contact the Commission on Colleges at 1866 Southern Lane, Decatur, Georgia 30033-4097 or call 404-679-4500 for questions about the accreditation of Montreat College. The College is approved to prepare students for elementary education teacher licensure by the North Carolina Department of Public Instruction (NC-DPI). The Master of Science in Environmental Education program is accredited by the North American Association for Environmental Education (NAAEE). Outdoor Education programs are accredited by the Wilderness Education Association and the Commission on Outdoor Education and Leadership.

Affiliation

Montreat College is a member of the Council for Christian Colleges and Universities, Appalachian College Association, Council of Independent Colleges, National Association of Independent Colleges and Universities, North Carolina Independent Colleges and Universities, Association of Christian Schools International, and National Association of Intercollegiate Athletics.

Undergraduate Academic Calendar for the School of Adult and Graduate Studies

Fall 2016

Event	Day	Date
Faculty Workshop (full-time faculty)	Tues-Wed	August 16-17
Fall Online Session 1 Course Add Deadline	Friday	August 26
Fall Session 1 Undergraduate Classes Begin	Sunday	August 28
Fall Session 1 Undergraduate Add/Drop Deadline	Sunday	September 4
Offices closed for Labor Day Holiday	Monday	September 5
Fall Session 1 Undergraduate Withdrawal with grade of W begins	Monday	September 5
Fall Session 1 Undergraduate Withdrawal with grade of WF begins	Monday	September 12
Fall Online Session 2 Course Add Deadline	Friday	September 30
Fall Session 1 Undergraduate Classes End	Saturday	October 1
Last day to apply for December graduation	Saturday	October 1
Fall Session 2 Undergraduate Classes Begin	Sunday	October 2
Homecoming and Family Weekend	Fri-Sat	Sept 30- Oct. 1
Grades for Fall Session 1 due before midnight	Saturday	October 8
Fall Session 2 Undergraduate Add/Drop Deadline	Sunday	October 9
Fall Session 2 Undergraduate Withdrawal with grade of W begins	Monday	October 10
Spring 2017 Registration Period Begins	Monday	October 17
Fall Session 2 Undergraduate Withdrawal with grade of WF begins	Monday	October 17
Board of Trustees meeting	Wed-Fri	October 12-14
Fall Online Session 3 Course Add Deadline	Friday	November 4
Fall Session 2 Undergraduate Classes End	Saturday	November 5
Fall Session 3 Undergraduate Classes Begins	Sunday	November 6
Grades for Fall Session 2 due before midnight	Saturday	November 12
Fall Session 3 Undergraduate Add/Drop Deadline	Sunday	November 13
Fall Session 3 Undergraduate Withdrawal with grade of W begins	Monday	November 14
Spring 2016 Registration Period Ends	Sunday	November 15
Fall Session 3 Undergraduate Withdrawal with grade of WF begins	Monday	November 21
Thanksgiving break - NO UNDERGRAD CLASSES	Sun-Sat	Nov. 20-26
College closed for Thanksgiving Holiday	Wed-Fri	Nov. 23-25
Spring 2017 Registration Period Ends	Sunday	November 27
December Commencement at 2 pm	Saturday	December 17
Fall Sessions 3 Undergraduate Classes End	Saturday	December 24
Christmas break - NO UNDERGRAD CLASSES	Sun-Sat	Dec 25-Jan. 7
College closed for Christmas Break	Fri-Mon	Dec 23-Jan. 2
Grades for Fall Session 3 due before midnight	Saturday	December 31
Deadline for last December graduation requirement	Saturday	December 31
December diploma conferral	Saturday	December 31

Graduate Academic Calendar for the School of Adult and Graduate Studies
Fall 2016

Event	Day	Date
Faculty Workshop (full-time faculty)	Tues-Wed	August 16-17
Fall Graduate Session 1 Online Course Deadline to Add	Friday	August 26
Fall Graduate Session 1 Classes Begin	Sunday	August 28
MSEE Fall Term Begins	Friday	September 2
Fall Graduate Session 1 Deadline to Add/Drop	Sunday	September 4
Fall Graduate Session 1 Withdrawal with grade of W begins	Monday	September 5
Offices closed for Labor Day Holiday (Mon. courses will meet)	Monday	September 5
MSEE Deadline to Add/Drop	Thursday	September 8
MSEE Withdrawal with a grade of W begins	Friday	September 9
Fall Graduate Session 1 Withdrawal with grade of WF begins	Monday	September 25
Last day to apply for December graduation	Saturday	October 1
Homecoming and Family Weekend	Fri-Sat	Sept 30-Oct 1
Board of Trustees meeting	Wed-Fri	October 12-14
Fall Graduate Session 2 Online Course Deadline to Add	Friday	October 21
Fall Graduate Session 1 Classes End	Saturday	October 22
Fall Graduate Session 2 Classes Begin	Sunday	October 23
MSEE Withdrawal with a grade of WF begins	Friday	October 28
Grades for Fall Graduate Session 1 due before midnight	Saturday	October 29
Fall Graduate Session 2 Deadline to Add/Drop Class	Sunday	October 30
Fall Graduate Session 2 Withdrawal with grade of W begins	Monday	October 31
Thanksgiving break - NO GRADUATE CLASSES	Sun-Sat	Nov 20-26
Fall Graduate Session 2 Withdrawal with grade of WF begins	Monday	November 21
College closed for Thanksgiving Holiday	Wed-Fri	Nov 23-25
December Commencement at 2 pm	Saturday	December 17
MSEE Fall Term Ends	Thursday	December 22
College closed for Christmas Break	Fri-Mon	Dec. 23-Jan. 2
Fall Graduate Session 2 Classes End	Saturday	December 24
Christmas break - NO GRADUATE CLASSES	Sun-Sat	Dec. 25-Jan 7
Grades for Fall Graduate Session 2 due before midnight	Saturday	December 31
Deadline for last December graduation requirement	Saturday	December 31
December degree conferral	Saturday	December 31

Undergraduate Academic Calendar for the School of Adult and Graduate Studies
Spring 2017

Event	Day	Date
Spring Online Session 1 Add Deadline	Friday	January 6
Spring Session 1 Undergraduate Classes Begin	Sunday	January 8
Faculty Workshop (full-time faculty)	Mon-Tue	January 9-10
Spring Session 1 Undergraduate Add/Drop Deadline	Sunday	January 15
Spring Session 1 Undergraduate Withdrawal with grade of W begins	Monday	January 16
Offices closed for Martin Luther King Day Holiday (Monday classes will meet)	Monday	January 16
Spring Session 1 Undergraduate Withdrawal with grade of WF begins	Monday	January 23
Board of Trustees meeting	Wed-Fri	January 25-27
Spring Online Session 2 Add Deadline	Friday	February 10
Spring Session 1 Undergraduate Classes End	Saturday	February 11
Spring Session 2 Undergraduate Classes Begin	Sunday	February 12
Grades for Spring Session 1 due before midnight	Saturday	February 18
Spring Session 2 Undergraduate Add/Drop Deadline	Sunday	February 19
Spring Session 2 Undergraduate Withdrawal with grade of W begins	Monday	February 20
Summer 2017 Registration Period Begins	Monday	February 20
Spring Session 2 Undergraduate Withdrawal with grade of WF begins	Monday	February 27
Last day to apply for May graduation	Wed	March 1
Spring Online Session 3 Add Deadline	Friday	March 17
Spring Session 2 Undergraduate Classes End	Saturday	March 18
Spring Session 3 Undergraduate Classes Begin	Sunday	March 19
Grades for Spring Session 2 due before midnight	Saturday	March 25
Spring Session 3 Undergraduate Add/Drop Deadline	Sunday	March 26
Spring Session 3 Undergraduate Withdrawal with grade of W begins	Monday	March 27
Summer 2017 Registration Period Ends	Sunday	March 26
Spring Session 3 Undergraduate Withdrawal with grade of WF begins	Monday	April 3
College closed for Easter Break	Fri-Mon	April 14-17
Easter break - NO UNDERGRAD CLASSES	Sun-Sat	Apr.16-22
Board of Trustees meeting	Wed-Fri	May 3-5
Spring Session 3 Undergraduate Classes End	Saturday	May 6
Grades for Spring Session 3 due before midnight	Saturday	May 13
Spring Commencement at 2 pm	Saturday	May 13
Deadline for last May graduation requirement	Wed	May 31
May degree conferral	Tuesday	May 31

Graduate Academic Calendar for the School of Adult and Graduate Studies
Spring 2017

Event	Day	Date
Spring Graduate Session 1 Online Course Deadline to Add	Friday	January 6
Spring Graduate Session 1 Classes Begin	Sunday	January 8
Faculty Workshop (full-time faculty)	Mon-Tue	January 9-10
Spring Graduate Session 1 Deadline to Add/Drop	Sunday	January 15
Spring Graduate Session 1 Withdrawal with grade of W begins	Monday	January 16
Offices closed for Martin Luther King Day (Monday classes meet)	Monday	January 16
Board of Trustees meeting	Wed-Fri	January 25-27
MSEE Spring Term Begins	Friday	January 27
MSEE Deadline to Add/Drop	Thursday	February 2
MSEE Withdrawal with grade of W begins	Friday	February 3
Spring Graduate Session 1 Withdrawal with grade of WF begins	Monday	February 6
Last day to apply for May graduation	Wed	March 1
Spring Graduate Session 2 Online Course Deadline to Add	Friday	March 3
Spring Graduate Session 1 Classes End	Saturday	March 4
Spring Graduate Session 2 Classes Begin	Sunday	March 5
Grades for Spring Graduate Session 1 due before midnight	Saturday	March 11
Spring Graduate Session 2 Deadline to Add/Drop	Sunday	March 12
Spring Graduate Session 2 Withdrawal with grade of W begins	Monday	March 13
MSEE Withdrawal with grade of WF begins	Friday	March 24
Spring Graduate Session 2 Withdrawal with grade of WF begins	Monday	April 3
College closed for Easter Break	Fri-Mon	April 14-17
Easter break - NO GRADUATE CLASSES	Sun-Sat	April 16-22
Board of Trustees meeting	Wed-Fri	May 3-5
Spring Graduate Session 2 Classes End	Saturday	May 6
Grades for Spring Graduate Session 2 due before midnight	Saturday	May 13
Spring Commencement at 2:00 p.m.	Saturday	May 13
MSEE Spring Term Ends	Thursday	May 18
Deadline for last May graduation requirement	Wed	May 31
May degree conferral	Wed	May 31

Undergraduate Academic Calendar for the School of Adult and Graduate Studies

Summer 2017

Event	Day	Date
Summer Online Session 1 Add Deadline	Friday	May 5
Summer Session 1 Undergraduate Classes Begin	Sunday	May 7
Summer Session 1 Undergraduate Add/Drop Deadline	Sunday	May 14
Summer Session 1 Undergraduate Withdrawal with grade of W begins	Monday	May 15
Summer Session 1 Undergraduate Withdrawal with grade of WF begins	Monday	May 22
Offices closed for Memorial Day (Monday classes will meet)	Monday	May 29
Last Day to apply for August graduation	Thursday	June 1
Summer Online Session 2 Add Deadline	Friday	June 9
Summer Session 1 Undergraduate Classes End	Saturday	June 10
Summer Session 2 Undergraduate Classes Begin	Sunday	June 11
Fall 2017 Registration Period Begins	Monday	June 12
Grades for Summer Session 1 due before midnight	Saturday	June 17
Summer Session 2 Undergraduate Add/Drop Deadline	Sunday	June 18
Summer Session 2 Undergraduate Withdrawal with grade of W begins	Monday	June 19
Summer Session 2 Undergraduate Withdrawal with grade of WF begins	Monday	June 26
Offices closed for Independence Day (Tuesday classes will meet)	Tuesday	July 4
Summer Online Session 3 Add Deadline	Friday	July 14
Summer Session 2 Undergraduate Classes End	Saturday	July 15
Summer Session 3 Undergraduate Classes Begin	Sunday	July 16
Grades for Summer Session 2 due before midnight	Saturday	July 22
Summer Session 3 Undergraduate Add/Drop Deadline	Sunday	July 23
Fall 2017 Registration Period Ends	Sunday	July 23
Summer Session 3 Undergraduate Withdrawal with grade of W begins	Monday	July 24
Summer Session 3 Undergraduate Withdrawal with grade of WF begins	Monday	July 31
Fall Online Session 1 Add Deadline	Friday	August 25
Summer Session 3 Undergraduate Classes End	Saturday	August 26
Fall Session 1 Undergraduate Classes Begin	Sunday	August 27
Deadline for last August graduation requirement	Thursday	August 31
August degree conferral	Thursday	August 31
Grades for Summer Session 3 due before midnight	Saturday	September 2

Graduate Academic Calendar for the School of Adult and Graduate Studies
Summer 2017

Event	Day	Date
Summer Graduate Session 1 Online Course Deadline to Add	Friday	May 5
Summer Graduate Session 1 Classes begin	Sunday	May 7
Summer Graduate Session 1 Deadline to Add/Drop	Sunday	May 14
Summer Graduate Session 1 Withdrawal with grade of W begins	Monday	May 15
MSEE Summer Term begins	Friday	May 19
MSEE Deadline to Add/Drop	Thursday	May 25
MSEE Withdrawal with grade of W begins	Friday	May 26
Offices closed for Memorial Day Holiday	Monday	May 29
Last Day to apply for August graduation	Thursday	June 1
Summer Graduate Session 1 Withdrawal with grade of WF begins	Monday	June 5
Summer Graduate Session 2 Online Course Deadline to Add	Friday	June 30
Summer Graduate Session 1 Classes End	Saturday	July 1
Summer Graduate Session 2 Classes Begin	Sunday	July 2
Offices closed for Independence Day Holiday	Tuesday	July 4
Grades for Summer Graduate Session 1 due before midnight	Saturday	July 8
Summer Graduate Session 2 Deadline to Drop	Sunday	July 9
Summer Graduate Session 2 Withdrawal with grade of W begins	Monday	July 10
MSEE Withdrawal with grade of WF begins	Friday	July 14
Summer Graduate Session 2 Withdrawal with grade of WF begins	Monday	July 31
Summer Graduate Session 2 Classes End	Saturday	August 26
Deadline for last August graduation requirement	Thursday	August 31
August diploma conferral	Wed.	August 31
MSEE Summer Term Ends	Thursday	August 31
Grades for Graduate Session 2 due before midnight	Saturday	September 2

About the School of Adult and Graduate Studies

The School of Adult and Graduate Studies seeks to provide education that is consistently informed by a Christian worldview to adult professionals with previous work experience. Program offerings permit working professionals to complete educational goals while fully involved in current careers. A special feature of this program is that working professionals can integrate their practical knowledge of the workplace with interactive classroom instruction and Christian principles.

The mission of the School of Adult and Graduate Studies is to provide compressed, experiential-based learning to adults with previous work experience. With an emphasis on group dynamics and interactive learning, the School of Adult and Graduate Studies integrates theory and practice and permits adults to complete their educational goals while continuing to be involved in their current career. Informed by a Christian worldview, the program is committed to promoting life-long learning with curricula that continually meet the needs of a changing work environment. Programs in the School of Adult and Graduate Studies are designed to meet the educational needs of working adults. The adult degree programs began in 1994 in Montreat, North Carolina. Currently, degree programs are offered throughout North Carolina with hundreds of students enrolled.

The School of Adult and Graduate Studies programs allow adults who want to advance their career opportunities a way to further their education through the Associate of Science (AS) degree; Bachelor of Business Administration (BBA) degree; Bachelor of Science in Management (BSM) degree; Bachelor of Science in Bible and Religion (BSBR) degree; Bachelor of Science in Psychology and Human Services (BSPHS) degree; Master of Arts in Clinical Mental Health Counseling (MACMHC) degree; Master of Business Administration (MBA) degree; Master of Science in Environmental Education (MSEE) degree; and Master of Science in Management and Leadership (MSML) degree. Programs are delivered in a non-traditional, accelerated format specifically designed for working adults who have work experience associated with their degree choice. Credentialed faculty members are carefully selected in order to provide appropriate instruction integrating theory with practical experience and Christian principles. Classes meet once a week for four-hour sessions of interactive instruction or online. Students may be required to meet once a week to complete such assigned group activities as presentations, research, and papers at the faculty's discretion.

Rights Reserved by the College

The College reserves the right to add or delete courses, to change academic policies, practices, and requirements, or to alter the academic catalog at any time. Courses with fewer than five students enrolled may be cancelled due to low enrollment.

By accepting admission into the College, a student is agreeing to abide by all official regulations of the College, including those published in this academic catalog. While this publication presents policies and programs as accurately as possible as of the date of publication, the College reserves the right to make such changes as future circumstances may require.

Admission Information

Undergraduate Admission Requirements

To qualify for admission into any Montreat College School of Adult and Graduate Studies undergraduate degree program, the following conditions must be satisfied:

- Applicants must be open to the College's mission of the integration of Christian faith and learning.
- Applicants must submit the following credentials:
  - Montreat College Application for Admission
  - Official, final transcripts of all college courses taken*
  - Official, final high school transcript or its equivalent (if transferring less than 12** semester credits of college credit)*
    - All final transcripts must include graduation information
  - Verification by the American Council on Education (ACE) of any eligible CLEP and DSST examinations, and non-collegiate military training.
- Applicants must have an overall grade point average (GPA) of 2.0 on a 4.0 scale or higher in all previous college work attempted. Only grades of C or above (2.0 on a 4.0 scale) are eligible for transfer consideration.

Applicants whose first language is not English must demonstrate the ability to read, write, and understand English and submit evidence of proficiency in English. See International Admission section for further explanation of requirements.

Individual consideration may be given to applicants who do not meet all the specific requirements. Students desiring this consideration must submit a letter to support their ability to succeed in the program. The College reserves the right to admit only students who hold promise of academic success. Withdrawal may be required should an applicant intentionally withhold or falsify pertinent information.

Once an applicant becomes a student, satisfactory academic progress must be maintained and will be reviewed three (3) times a year while enrolled at Montreat College.

Students wishing to complete an associate degree while pursuing a bachelor degree must have the two-year degree conferred at least one academic year prior to earning the four-year degree.

*Admissions decisions may be made based on unofficial transcript(s). However, all required final, official transcripts must be received by the end of the first course taken at Montreat College. If these are not received, the student will be withdrawn immediately. Any Montreat College charges incurred by the withdrawal date are the responsibility of the student.

**Students using Veteran's Affairs Educational Benefits are required to have an official high school transcript sent prior to full admission for students transferring less than 24 semester credits. VA students' courses and fees cannot be certified until these are received.

AGS Undergraduate Degrees

The Associate of Science (AS) provides a solid foundation in the arts and sciences in addition to introductory courses in a chosen concentration of business or general studies. Upon completion of the program, students are able to explain the basic principles of their concentration, demonstrate critical thinking skills, and use effective oral and written communication techniques.

The Bachelor of Business Administration (BBA) provides a valuable balance of theory and practical experience, preparing students to work effectively in today's complex business environment. The program promotes immediate implementation of classroom theory to the work environment.
The Bachelor of Business Administration degree program offers three concentrations from which to choose: General Business, Human Resource Management, and Marketing.

> **General Business (GB)** concentration continues the student's journey through different areas of the business world. Graduates will have a wide variety of skills, from Administrative Theory to Strategic Management, to add to their work experience or preparation to continue their education at the graduate level.

> **Human Resource Management (HRM)** concentration helps students develop an understanding of the fundamentals of human resource management and its relevance in business. The concentration addresses the legal and ethical components of the decision making process involved in the human resources environment.

> **Marketing (MKT)** concentration prepares students for a career in all aspects of marketing; how to identify customer needs, how to communicate information about products and services to customers and potentials customers, where to market, and the pricing of products and services.

The Bachelor of Science in Bible and Religion (BSBR) prepares students for graduate studies and/or church ministry. Students will receive instruction in biblical studies and theology as well as practical training in preaching, spiritual formation, and church administration.

The Bachelor of Science in Bible and Religion is offered with the following concentration:

> **Preaching and Evangelism (P&E)** concentration is focused on preaching and teaching the message of the Gospel. This course of study gives students a basic understanding of Christian scripture and theology and will be supplemented by the use of online courses in preparing and preaching the gospel of Jesus Christ produced by the Billy Graham Evangelistic Association. The required coursework attempts to blend both an academic and practical approach to church ministry.

The Bachelor of Science in Management (BSM) provides solid instruction in managerial and leadership principles and theory with a focus on developing the leadership competencies required in today's work environment, both private and public. The BSM degree is comprehensive and does not require students to choose a concentration. However, students have the option of adding a concentration to their degree by completing the coursework required for one of the following BBA concentrations: Cybersecurity, Human Resource Management, or Marketing.

The Bachelor of Science in Psychology and Human Services (BSPHS) equips students with the knowledge, skills, and experience they need for working in social agencies, churches, and other settings, as well as preparing students to enter graduate programs in psychology, counseling, and social work. This curriculum will engage a course of study that focuses on psychological theories and research about human behavior and psychological processes with an emphasis on developing and implementing skills for helping individuals and families face the challenges of our present society.

Graduate Degree Admission Requirements

To qualify for admission into any Montreat College School of Adult and Graduate Studies graduate degree program, the following conditions must be satisfied:

- Applicants must have openness to the College's mission of the integration of Christian faith and learning.
- An applicant must meet the following conditions:
  - Submit a Montreat College Application for Admission
  - Have a baccalaureate degree from a regionally accredited college or university.
  - Provide official final transcripts showing completion of a baccalaureate degree, showing the last 60 hours of undergraduate study, and any undergraduate pre-requisite courses needed for the graduate degree program.*
  - Provide official final transcripts for any graduate level coursework completed.*
- In addition to the above requirements, students applying for graduate admission must also meet the requirements specific to their intended program of study.

Applicants whose first language is not English must demonstrate the ability to read, write, and understand English and submit evidence of proficiency in English. See International Admission section for further explanation of requirements.

Individual consideration may be given to applicants who do not meet all the specific requirements. Students desiring this consideration must submit additional credentials to support their ability to succeed in the program. The College reserves the right to admit only students who hold promise of academic success. Withdrawal may be required should an applicant intentionally withhold or falsify pertinent information.

*Admissions decisions may be made based on unofficial transcript(s). However, all required final, official transcripts must be received by the end of the first course taken at Montreat College. If these are not received, the student will be withdrawn immediately. Students receiving Veteran's Affairs benefits cannot be certified for courses or fees until these transcripts are received. Any Montreat College charges incurred by the withdrawal date are the responsibility of the student.

AGS Graduate Degrees

The Master of Arts in Clinical Mental Health Counseling (MACMHC) educates students in the history and development of the counseling profession, the theories of counseling, the ethical practice of counseling, the competencies required for working with multicultural and diverse groups, and the strategies for working with individuals across the lifespan in everyday developmental, behavioral, psychological, social, emotional, and career challenges and crisis. Further, the program prepares candidates to become competent counselor practitioners who are life-long learners, critical thinkers, agents of social justice in their communities, and spokespersons for transformation, renewal, and reconciliation in their spheres of influence, within the conceptual framework of Counselor as Advocate, Leader, and Collaborator.

The Master of Science in Environmental Education (MSEE) deepens students' understanding of environmental issues from a variety of perspectives while working in a cohort with other professionals in the field. Students become well-rounded researchers and educators, learning effective strategies for environmental education and strengthening their science knowledge. This program complements the College's Environmental Studies and Outdoor Education undergraduate programs while meeting environmental education needs in the State. The curriculum has been developed in connection with the North Carolina State Environmental Education Certification program.

The Master of Business Administration (MBA) provides graduate-level training in the theory and practice of contemporary business management with practical application from domestic and global perspectives. Students gain the leadership and analytical skills necessary for managerial success in both public and private industry.

The Master of Science in Management and Leadership (MSML) is a natural progression from the BSM program and provides adult learners with tools and skills needed to excel as managers and leaders. Coursework has a qualitative focus that progresses from developing the individual's leadership foundation to building relationships between organizational members and stakeholders to determining strategy for a range of organizations. Students do not need a business background, just a determination for leadership regardless of positional authority.

Master of Arts in Clinical Mental Health Counseling (MACMHC)

To qualify for admission into the Master of Arts in Clinical Mental Health Counseling degree program, the following conditions must be *satisfied in addition to the standard graduate admissions requirements*:

- Have a minimum cumulative GPA of 3.0 from the last 60 credit hours of undergraduate study*
- Submit a Professional Goals Essay
- Submit a current resume that includes both academic and employment history
- Submit official transcripts for *all* colleges attended (this may include additional transcripts beyond the standard graduate admissions requirements)
- Submit GRE scores**
- Meet GRE/GPA Formula Scores:

Minimum combined score of 290, with 2.5 writing score, on the GRE.
Minimum undergraduate GPA of 3.0 (on a 4.0 scale) on last 60 hours.
Minimum formula score of 1,490 [(400 X GPA) + GRE]

- Complete and pay for a national background check
- Complete a personal interview with the Program Director and other panel members

*If applicant has a cumulative GPA below 3.0, a "Low GPA" essay is required. The essay should cover challenges that contributed to the low GPA, as well as specifically what the applicant will do to maintain a 3.0 overall GPA in the CMHC program.

**GRE Scores are only valid for 5 years. GRE requirement is waived under two circumstances:
1. The applicant has completed a master's degree in full and is verified by receipt of official transcripts
2. The applicant is applying as a transfer student with graduate level counseling coursework or from a counseling degree program that did not require the GRE for admissions and provides proof.

Master of Science in Environmental Education (MSEE)

To qualify for admission into the Master of Science in Environmental Education degree program, the following conditions must be satisfied *in addition to the graduate admissions requirements*:

- Have a minimum GPA of 3.0 from the last 60 credit hours of undergraduate study.
- Submit a cover letter and resume that includes both academic and employment history.
- Submit an Admissions Essay.
- Submit two (2) letters of recommendation. Letters should include a statement about how the reference perceives that the applicant will do in graduate school.

Master of Science in Management and Leadership (MSML)

To qualify for admission into the Master of Science in Management and Leadership degree program, the following conditions must be *satisfied in addition to the graduate admissions requirements*:

- Have a minimum cumulative GPA of 2.75 from the last 60 credit hours of undergraduate study
- Submit an Applicant Essay

Master of Business Administration (MBA)

To qualify for admission into the Master of Business Administration degree program, the following condition must be satisfied *in addition to the graduate admissions requirements*:

- Meet the following GMAT* score requirement: **(GPA x 200) + GMAT ≥ 950**

*Montreat College waives the GMAT entrance examination for any graduate from a regionally accredited college or university with an undergraduate degree in Business and a 3.0 grade point average (last 60 hours), who begins the program within three years of degree conferral.

NOTE: The Graduate Management Admission Test (GMAT) score must be official and completed within the last five (5) years.

Applicants must fulfill all undergraduate business prerequisites before taking the corresponding MBA courses. (Individuals with a BBA degree from Montreat College School of Adult and Graduate Studies will have already completed all the necessary undergraduate prerequisites). Candidates for the MBA degree will be required to successfully complete (with a grade of C or higher) the following prerequisite undergraduate business courses*:

- BS 352 Financial Accounting Issues: 3 credit hours (intermediate level accounting)
- BS 422 Issues in Corporate Finance: 3 credit hours
- BS 351 Economics Theory, Concepts, and Issues of Micro and Macro: 3 credit hours (or both Micro and Macro at the 200-level)
- MT 122 Elementary Statistics: 3 credit hours

*Prerequisites for the MBA program are offered through the School of Adult and Graduate Studies. Prerequisites may also be fulfilled by equivalent courses from a regionally accredited college or university (official transcript showing proof must be submitted to Montreat College).

Readmission of Former Students

Students formerly enrolled at Montreat College who, for any reason, have not attended classes within one academic year or officially withdrew from their academic program must submit the following:

- A readmission application.

- Students who have been enrolled at another institution and are applying for readmission to Montreat College must submit an official transcript from each institution attended since leaving Montreat College.

- Students applying for readmission to Montreat College who have been withdrawn from Montreat College for one full year or more are held to all requirements of the current Academic Catalog at the time of readmission.

- Any undergraduate student readmitting to Montreat College must have minimum combined GPA of 2.0 on a 4.0 scale for all academic work completed while at Montreat College and at any other institution during the time since attending Montreat College.

- Any graduate student readmitting to Montreat College must have a minimum combined graduate GPA of 3.0 on a 4.0 scale for all academic work completed while a at Montreat College and at any other institutions during the time since attending Montreat College.

- Students who have left Montreat College either on Academic Probation or Academic Suspension must submit a letter of appeal addressed to the Admissions Committee explaining the circumstance that led to the probation or suspension and why the student will now be academically successful. The Admissions Committee may request an interview or other requirements prior to making an admission determination. If granted readmission, these students will enter Montreat College on Academic Probation and be subject to the academic policies as stated in the catalog.

- Students who have been suspended due to academic dishonesty will not be eligible to reapply to Montreat College for at least two (2) years after dismissal. Students who have been suspended for dishonesty and wish to be readmitted must write a letter of appeal for readmission after meeting all other readmission requirements. This letter should be addressed to the Vice President and Dean for Adult and Graduate Studies.

- All students being readmitted should contact the Financial Aid and Student Accounts offices as soon as possible to ensure their student account is cleared and their financial aid application is complete.
- Students with outstanding balances with Montreat College must clear their account with the Business Office before being allowed to attend class.

A decision regarding readmission for all Adult and Graduate Studies degree programs is made by the Office of Admission.

For more information about readmission to the Montreat College School of Adult and Graduate Studies, please contact the Office of Admission or visit the Montreat College website at www.montreat.edu to reapply for admission.

Admission of Non-Degree Seeking Students

Non-Degree students may be admitted to the College to take up to 12 total academic hours without pursuing a degree.

Special student classifications include the following:
- Visiting=degree-seeking at another institution
- Non-degree=receiving college credit but not seeking a degree
- Audit=attending college course without receiving credit

Students wishing to enter under the non-degree classification should submit the following:

- A non-degree seeking student application A non-degree seeking student application
- An official transcript showing good academic standing from the last institution attended or a letter to that effect from the institution.
- Additional official transcript showing the completion of pre-requisite or co-requisite courses, if planning to enroll in courses for which these are required.

Students who are non-degree seeking are not eligible for financial aid.

A student wishing to take more than 12 credits must apply as a regular student through the Office of Admission.

All 12 credits earned while a non-degree seeking student can be applied toward a degree program with Montreat College.

Evaluation of Transfer Credit

Students will receive an evaluation of their transfer credit upon acceptance to the College. This evaluation is a summary of the number of semester credits accepted in transfer from all regionally accredited colleges and universities, proficiency examinations the student has previously completed, and military training. If requested, students will be provided a copy of the official evaluation once accepted by the Office of Records and Registration.

Conditions of Acceptance of Transfer Credit

Montreat College strives to ensure the highest quality academic experience for all students. Therefore, the College limits the number and type of transfer credits accepted. The College requires that credits apply to students' degree programs and limit the number of credits applied via credit-by-examination, from non-regionally accredited institutions, and from documented learning. Similarly, Montreat College does not accept transfer credits acquired through groups that lack appropriate approval by the American Council on Education.

- Academic work from a regionally accredited school with a grade of *C* or better (2.00 on a 4.00 scale) for undergraduate courses and a grade of *B* or better (3.00 on a 4.00 scale) for graduate courses will be accepted in transfer. Courses that do not apply to a student's degree program will not be accepted.
- Undergraduate students may transfer up to 2 physical education activity courses in which they received a *P* (passing credit). These are the only courses where a grade of *P* is acceptable for transfer credit.
- Transferred courses must be at the same level and be equivalent in content to the Montreat College courses. If there is any question of course equivalency, it is the responsibility of the student to provide proof that courses are equivalent (i.e. provide course descriptions, syllabus).
- Montreat College endorses the North Carolina Comprehensive Articulation Agreement, which can be viewed at www.northcarolina.edu. Transfer students who have earned the Associate in Arts or Associate in Science degree from a North Carolina Community College and who meet the minimum requirements for admission to Montreat College will receive transfer credit for all eligible courses subject to normal transfer credit policy. No more than **66** semester hours may be transferred from two-year schools.
- The maximum number of undergraduate credits that may transfer from other institutions is **90** semester credits.
- The maximum number of graduate credits that may transfer to a Montreat College graduate program is **6** semester credits, with the exception of the CMHC program which allows **9** semester credits in transfer (see CMHC program handbook for more information).

- The combined total of credits that can be accepted from non-regionally accredited colleges or universities, NCA credit, or Credits by Examination is **30** for a bachelor degree, or **15** for an associate degree.
  - Courses from non-regionally accredited colleges or universities are considered on a course-by-course basis; coursework must have an earned grade of *C* or better; *acceptance of such credits is dependent upon Montreat College's evaluation of the equivalency of coursework and level of instruction*.
    - Academic work presented from a nationally accredited agency recognized by the Council for Higher Education Accreditation may be evaluated for transfer equivalency.
    - Students may request that academic work presented from a non-accredited faith-related institution be considered for transfer equivalency. Courses will be reviewed with the potential for **6** total credits allowed in transfer.
- For courses from an international institution, the transcript must be translated and evaluated by a credible educational evaluation company.
- The transfer of courses into the undergraduate or graduate core must be approved by the Office of Records and Registration, in consultation with a full-time faculty member in the discipline. Approval of transfer credit for the program core should be finalized prior to enrollment into the degree program.
- Credits from regionally accredited institutions will be considered for a course that Montreat College offers no equivalent course, provided that the transferred course is considered within the general framework of the liberal arts curriculum and is relevant to the degree pursued. Only courses that are academic in nature and purpose will be accepted in transfer.
- Vocational training courses such as air-conditioning technology, electrical circuitry, welding, and typing are not accepted. However, some vocational courses that are academic in content may be considered for transfer credits up to 30 semester credits.
- Transferred quarter credit hours will be converted to semester credits using the following formula: **Semester credit = quarter hours x 2/3.**
- A degree-seeking Montreat College student who wishes to enroll in courses offered by another institution must complete the required form and receive approval to do so from the Office of Records and Registration. Failure to follow this procedure may result in loss of transfer credit for these courses.
- Students transferring with senior status from another institution must successfully complete at least **18** semester credit hours in their major and a minimum of **32** credits overall at Montreat College.
- Courses transferred to Montreat College will be assigned the grade of *P* (passing) and will be considered as earned credit but will not affect the grade point average or graduation honors.

International Admission

International applicants must be graduates of a secondary school system or the equivalent and must have sufficient proficiency in the English language to be able to study at the college level.

International students must submit the following:

- A Montreat College application for admission.
- An official, translated transcript of the student's secondary school record, preferably indicating class rank and GPA. Montreat College requires that the applicant use a transcript translation and evaluation service in order to determine international academic credentials. Acceptable transcript translation and evaluation services include World Education Services, www.wes.org; AACRAO International Education Services, www.aacrao.org; and International Education Evaluations, Inc., www.foreigntranscripts.com.
- Applicants whose first language is not English must demonstrate the ability to read, write, and understand English and submit evidence of proficiency in English. The applicant must either transfer in the undergraduate English composition requirements from another English-speaking higher education institution; meet the minimum Test of English as a Foreign Language (TOEFL) score requirements of a minimum score of 67 on the internet-based exam, 187 on the computer-based exam, or 517 on the paper-based exam; or have an overall band score of 6 on the Test Report Form (TRF) from the International English Language Testing System (IELTS). Applicants who speak English as a second language must submit official results for whichever requirement above is applicable.

Credit By Examination

Adult learners may participate in a variety of credit by examination programs in order to earn credit toward the associate or bachelor degree. Credit will be transferred as pass/fail. No credit will be granted for an exam for which the student failed to meet the exam minimum score. Some tests may be taken only one time; other tests may be taken one time in a six-month period. These programs are explained below.

Credits by examination are not eligible for financial aid on their own and do not count as in-class status for enrollment purposes. Financial aid is not awarded for these credits. If examination credit is used to replace a course for which financial aid has been awarded, the aid for that course will be removed from the account. All students using credit by examination to complete their degree requirements must have completed all testing two months prior to the graduation date.

Advanced Placement (AP) Exams
https://apstudent.collegeboard.org/home
This credit by examination program is sponsored by the College Entrance Examination Board for evidence of completion of a college-level course taken in high school. Scores of 3, 4, or 5 will be accepted.

College Level Examination Program (CLEP)
www.collegeboard.com
The CLEP subject area examination will award credit toward graduation to students who received a passing score on the exam according to ACE recommendations. To have your scores sent to Montreat College, use school code 5423.

Defense Activity for Nontraditional Education Support (DSST)
www.getcollegecredit.com
This credit by examination program uses various subject area examinations. Guidelines developed by the American Council on Education (ACE) for awarding these credits are followed.

International Baccalaureate (IB): The International Baccalaureate Organization's Diploma Program is a demanding two year, pre-university course of study that leads to examinations. It is designed for highly motivated secondary school students aged 16 to 19. Similar to Advanced Placement (AP) examinations, students enrolled in the International Baccalaureate (IB) Diploma Program earn credit hours or advanced placement in college courses. Scores of 5 or 6 will be accepted, depending on the discipline.

ECE: http://www.excelsior.edu/registering-for-exams
This credit by examination program is similar to other subject area examinations. Guidelines developed by the American Council on Education (ACE) for awarding these credits are followed.

Students interested in taking one of these exams should contact an academic advisor at their campus location. Before taking any credit by examination exam, a prior approval form, available at any campus, must be completed to ensure the credit will apply toward the degree program as intended by the student. If credit by examination exams have been taken prior to enrollment, the student must request official score transcripts from the examination program and have them sent to Montreat College.

Credit for Montreat College will not be based upon academic credit awarded by another institution.

The combined total NCA Credits and Credits by Examination are limited to a total of 15 semester credits for an associate degree and 30 semester credits for a bachelor degree.

Assessment of Documented Learning

Those seeking elective credit for professional experience have two options at their disposal: (1) Non-collegiate Credit Assessment (NCA), which is an evaluation of certified corporate training; and (2) military credit. Both programs are designed to assist undergraduate-level students in earning credits for past or ongoing training at their place of employment. Specific policies and fees are associated with these programs and students need to be aware of their responsibilities as they utilize these programs.

Note: All military information must be received at the time of application. Montreat College closely follows the American Council of Education (ACE) recommendations. Students may have certain certifications or professional training experiences, but this does not mean they are awarded credit. If an exact or comparable match to the certification cannot be found in the ACE recommendations, Montreat College will not award academic credit. Any ACE recommendation must also meet the criteria for collegiate transfer credit (see Conditions of Acceptance of Transfer Credit).

Non-collegiate Credit Assessment (NCA)

Students should submit requests for Non-collegiate Credit Assessment (NCA) for activities undertaken prior to enrollment at Montreat College to their academic advisor during their **first three (3) months of enrollment**. Once enrolled at Montreat College, all (NCA) evaluation packets for newly completed job training evaluation, are due **three (3) months after completing training**. In order to begin the NCA evaluation process, the following five (5) items are required and must be submitted to your Academic Advisor.

- Official and original certificate of completion for each course to be evaluated. Certificates will be returned to students upon completion of the evaluation.
- A content description of each course to be evaluated. This must be an official course description such as the course brochure.
- Contact hour verification for each course to be evaluated. This must be from an official source such as a company's human resources department, official certificate, or course description. Contact hours are the number of hours spent in class for the course. As a general rule, for a course to be considered for college credit, it must have a minimum of 15 contact hours.
- A 2- to 4-page competency paper containing a detailed summary of what was gained from the course and how it applies to professional as well as private life. A paper is required for each course to be evaluated.
- A nonrefundable evaluation fee of $35 payable to Montreat College. The evaluation fee will be applied toward the first hour of credit if at least one hour of credit is awarded. The fee for additional credit hours awarded is **$35 per credit hour. NCA packets not containing the evaluation fee will be returned**.

The contact hour verification and competency paper may be waived if the student can have an official ACE (American Council of Education) transcript sent directly to Montreat College School of Adult and Graduate Studies.
Current NCA being used to meet graduation deadlines must be submitted no later than the deadline for the graduation application.

Note:
- Allow three (3) to four (4) weeks after receipt of all the above material for an evaluation to be completed. Credit awarded will be posted to the Montreat College transcript once the Office of Records and Registration has notification of the results and fee payment.
- Exams must be taken by the end of the month of the graduation application deadline: March 31 for Spring, June 30 for Summer and October 31 for Fall.
- The combined total NCA Credits and Credits by Examination are limited to a total of 15 semester credits for an associate degree and 30 semester credits for a bachelor degree. NCA credits may only be awarded as elective credits toward graduation.

Military Credit

Military credit is treated in the same way as general transfer credit. Military credits may count toward specific course requirements beyond general electives. Following the review of military transcripts by the Office of Enrollment and the Office of Records and Registration, academic department chairs will be consulted to review courses for major-specific transfer credit.

Montreat College uses the American Council on Education's (ACE) guide to evaluate educational experiences in the armed services for evaluating all military credit. An official *Joint Services Transcript* (JST) or officially certified DD-214 is carefully evaluated for all details concerning military experiences; credits are awarded at face value. The JST should accompany the student's application for admission; however, awarded credits may not be counted toward admission requirements. The ACE recommendation for use of military credit(s) must fit within a Montreat College program for transfer credit to be approved. Credits can be applied to the major if they closely match Montreat College courses.

Credits completed at the Community College of the Air Force with a grade of *S* are reviewed as general elective credit. Credits with grades of *A – C* are evaluated just like any other 2-year college transcript.

Articulation Agreements

Montreat College School of Adult and Graduate Studies endorses the North Carolina College System Comprehensive Articulation Agreement. For a more detailed explanation of this agreement, contact your academic advisor at your campus location.

The Montreat College School of Adult and Graduate Studies has also signed individual articulation agreements with certain North Carolina higher education institutions for particular degree programs. For information on institution to institution articulation agreements, please see the academic advising staff.

Student Accounts Office

Montreat College endeavors to provide an opportunity for Christian higher education to all who desire it. By working to keep expenses at a minimum and by offering a substantial and comprehensive financial aid program, the College provides an educational opportunity for many students who otherwise might not be financially able to attend college.

Questions about the Student Accounts Office may be directed to:

Montreat College
School of Adult and Graduate Studies (AGS)
800-436-2777 or 828-669-8012 ext. 1019
www.montreat.edu/studentaccounts
agsstudentaccounts@montreat.edu

Tuition and Fee Structure

Tuition and fees for the School of Adult and Graduate Studies are structured by degree program.

Tuition rates *per credit hour* are:

Undergraduate:	$395.00
Graduate: Counseling	$435.00
Graduate: Business Administration	$510.00
Graduate: Management and Leadership	$510.00
Graduate: Environmental Education	see chart below

Graduate: Environmental Education	Per Semester	Total Per Program
Technology Fee	$35.00	$175.00
Lab Fees (first three semesters)	$1,000.00	$3,000.00
Tuition per semester (5 semesters)	$4,104.00	$20,520.00
Total Tuition and Fees per Program		$23,695.00**

**Additionally, enrollment in EV 570 (Non-resident Thesis; $500 per semester) is required until a student completes all program requirements.

NOTE: Tuition does *not* include books.

42

Applicable Fees:

- All students are charged a technology fee of $35.00 per semester.

- Course by Arrangement (CBA) fee: $50.00 per credit hour.

- A $60.00 Graduation Fee is due upon filing the graduation application for all degree programs.

- The cost to audit an undergraduate class is $100.00. To audit a graduate class the cost is $200.00. The student is responsible for purchasing of required textbooks.

- Students who withdraw from and reenter any program must adhere to the prevailing standards and fee structures at the time of reentry. Any changes to scheduling may also affect the amount and timing of financial aid available.

- All outstanding balances must be cleared before future course or program registrations will be approved. The College reserves the right to withdraw students from a course for failure to meet financial obligations. A $50 late fee is charged each time a payment is received after the due date. There is a $25 charge for any check returned for insufficient funds.

Montreat College reserves the right to modify any of the above charges at any time.

Tuition Reimbursements

Students who anticipate that all or part of their expenses will be paid by employer tuition reimbursement are expected to pay in advance for courses with their own funds.

Receipt Requests

Students may request receipts for reimbursement purposes by submitting a receipt request form to agsstudentaccounts@montreat.edu. The form is available at www.montreat.edu/studentaccounts on the "Forms" page.

Student Accounts Statements

The Student Accounts Office sends statements to all students with a balance each term, as a courtesy. Not receiving a statement does not excuse the student from paying their balance. It is the responsibility of the student to pay their balance on time and courses will be dropped for late/non-payment. Students may view their accounts online using Self-Service; the link and instructions are available at www.montreat.edu/studentaccounts. Statements are not routinely sent to students with a zero (0) or credit balance.

Payment of Tuition and Fees

Self-Pay: (non-financial aid recipient-not applying for Federal loans/grants or State grants by completing a FAFSA)

Tuition and fees are due at least two weeks prior to the start of each class. The final day to make payment is the Wednesday prior to the start of each **session**, or the course may be dropped for non-payment.   A late payment penalty of $50 will be assessed if payment is not made by the class start date. Classes may be dropped for non-payment.

Financial Aid recipients – All required financial aid paperwork/documents are required to be submitted to the Financial Aid Department by the third class meeting. If paperwork/ documents are not received by the third class meeting all remaining courses/schedule may be dropped.

At the time a student formally registers for classes, either by signing and submitting the appropriate registration forms to the Student Services Office or by registering online through the website, when available, the student agrees to abide by the College's official policies concerning the adding and dropping of classes and/or the complete withdrawal from Montreat College. Dropping classes after the last drop/add date will not result in a refund of charges or fees. The student also agrees to assume responsibility for understanding the College's official policy concerning schedule changes and satisfactory academic progress which may result in additional charges or the loss of eligibility for certain types of financial aid. It is considered the student's responsibility to understand how these changes can affect his/her financial situation with regard to financial aid eligibility. Students should view their accounts online using Self-Service; the link and directions are available at www.montreat.edu/studentaccounts.

If an account must be sent to a collection agency or be litigated due to nonpayment of the outstanding balance, the College reserves the right to demand payment in full of subsequent terms of enrollment, prior to the beginning of each term to ensure enrollment. The College reserves the right to cancel the registration of any student if a balance due from a previous term remains unpaid at the start of a subsequent term.

Student receivable accounts are considered to be educational loans provided for the sole purpose of financing an education at Montreat College, a non-profit institution of higher learning. As such, student receivable accounts are not dischargeable under the provisions of the laws governing either Chapter 7 or Chapter 13 bankruptcy actions.

The College reserves the right to demand payment in the forms of a certified check, money order, cash, or credit cards in the event that one or more checks have been returned unpaid for any reason.

Students who have unpaid accounts or other outstanding obligations at the College will not be eligible to register for classes nor return for the next term. Transcripts, certificates and diplomas are not issued unless all charges have been paid in full. The College reserves the right to recover all costs involved with the collection and/or litigation of delinquent accounts as well as levy an interest charge equal to one and one half percent (1.5%) per month, on any account with a balance beyond thirty days past due. Student accounts are assessed fines for overdue library books, damaged property, parking violations, etc., as those charges are incurred.

General Institutional Student Accounts Policy

The payment of all tuition and fees becomes an obligation upon registration at Montreat College (hereafter referred to as "the College"). The Federal Truth-in-Lending Act requires complete disclosure of the terms and conditions controlling payment of the student's obligations. In order to comply with those federal statutes and regulations, the College discloses billing policies in the Academic Catalog and requests that the student carefully review the following:

Prior to the completion of registration, the student shall pay any prior obligations due on his/her account. An account that has a delinquent balance at the time the student schedules classes for the following semester prohibits the student from completing the registration process until the account is paid in full. Payment is due in full after registration and prior to the start of each course. Any changes in the student's financial obligations caused by a change in schedule or in aid are available for the student to view using Self-Service on the Montreat College website. The College reserves the right offer monthly payment plans on past due accounts, and to terminate said arrangement for non-payment. In the event of such a termination, the entire balance shall be immediately due and payable. The student's failure to pay the entire balance within 30 days shall result in the account being handled as a delinquent account as explained below.

Delinquent accounts occur when the payment terms on a student's account have not been met. When an account becomes delinquent, a billing statement is sent giving two weeks to make payment in full. If payment is not made, a statement will be sent giving an additional two weeks to make payment or the account will be sent to an external collection agency. The College has the right to take steps to collect the balance, including but not limited to the following: dropping the student from courses, prohibiting registration for future courses, withholding course credits, academic transcripts and diplomas until the balance is paid; turning over the student's account to a collection agency; and taking legal action to collect the balance due.

In addition, students may be removed from current course enrollment. The student authorizes the College to release financial information about his/her account to those concerned with collecting the balance owing. If the College incurs any expenses in collecting the student's account, the student shall pay all the College's cost of collection. This includes, but is not limited to, a collection agency fee, interest, and/or reasonable attorney's fees. In the event that appropriate tuition and fees are not paid and the college is forced to take formal collection procedures, the party or parties liable for such unpaid tuition will further be liable to the College for reasonable attorney's fees, plus all other reasonable expenses incurred by the College in collecting the delinquency, to the extent allowed by law.

The student is financially responsible for tuition and fees. <u>The student will not be held responsible for the balance of the course charges and required/ applicable fees if the College receives a written notice of withdrawal before the first day classes begin.</u> Financial Aid will be adjusted/reduced according to Federal guidelines.

General Institutional Withdrawal Policy

The following refund policy will be in effect for students enrolled in standard Terms:
- If a student drops* a course before the first week of class or during the drop/add period, the student will not be charged for tuition or fees.
- If a student withdraws* from a course after the last drop/add date, the student will be charged the full tuition rate and fees for that course.

The following refund policy will be in effect for students enrolled in non-standard Terms.
- If a student drops* a course before the second class meeting, the student will not be charged for tuition, but will be charged a $50.00 drop/add processing fee.
- If a student withdraws* from a course after the second class meeting, the student will be charged the full tuition rate and fees for that course.

*It is the responsibility of the student to officially drop a course by notifying her or his academic advisor and completing a properly executed Drop/Add Form. If a form is not submitted, the student will be charged in full for the course and related fees, and the student will earn a grade for the course, or in the case of non-attendance, a WF.

All past due amounts, including such charges as tuition, bookstore charges, library fines, student fees, etc., are subject to a 1.5% per month finance charge. Students will not be issued official grade transcripts or permitted to register for succeeding semesters until such time all fees have been paid in full. Diplomas will not be issued unless all fees have been satisfied.

Refund/Repayment Policy

If the student withdraws from the College, then the General Institutional Withdrawal Policy will apply.

A student is considered enrolled for attendance purposes until the last day of attendance or the end of the term, whichever is first. To withdraw from courses, the student should follow the formal withdrawal process outlined in this catalog. Official withdrawal forms are available from an Academic Advisor or from the Office of Records and Registration.

A refund refers to money paid toward college charges that must be returned to financial aid sources and/or the student. A repayment is the amount of cash disbursed to the student that must be repaid to federal, state, or institutional sources. The amount of refund will depend upon whether the student has received Federal Title IV and/or state financial assistance.

Return of Title IV Student Aid

In the event a student withdraws or is administratively withdrawn from the College, the Financial Aid Office is required to process a withdrawal calculation. Such a calculation is based upon the student's last date of documented class attendance. All awards that include Federal Title IV aid will be subject to the Federal Return of Title IV Funds calculation. All State funds will be subject to State requirements to determine award eligibility. All other nonfederal funds are subject to the Montreat College withdrawal calculation. Montreat College has a fair and equitable refund policy, as required under Section 668.22(b)(1) of the federal regulations.

The Federal Return of Title IV Funds calculation determines the percentage of the period of enrollment for which the assistance was awarded. This figure is used to determine the percentage of aid the student earned for the period of enrollment, based on the number of days actually completed. All unearned funds are returned to the proper agencies in the order prescribed by federal and state laws: Unsubsidized Direct Loan; Subsidized Direct Loan, Federal GRAD PLUS Loan; Federal Pell Grant; other state, private, or institutional aid; the student. **Students must pay any charges remaining on their account after funds are returned to the proper agencies.**

Credit Balances

Students may receive a refund of a credit balance from their account during the term, though not prior to the conclusion of the first week of the term or the **actual receipt of the financial funds**. All Funds Requests forms must be submitted by 12 p.m. Thursday to be processed for the following Wednesday check run. The check will be mailed to the current address on file within 14 business days. If a request is denied an email notification/explanation will be sent to the student's Montreat College email. Forms may only be sent from a student's Montreat College email to: agsstudentaccounts@montreat.edu, or by e-fax at: 828-419-2298. The AGS Funds Request form can be located at http://www.montreat.edu/student-accounts/forms/.

If a student's address is different than what is on file the student must submit a Student Information Change form to the Office of Records and Registration before a check will be mailed. The form may be obtained at www.montreat.edu/registrar-office/forms or from an Advisor. Withdrawals from the student's account will be based on information that is currently available to the Student Accounts and Financial Aid Offices. If financial aid changes or additional charges are added to the account, the student will be responsible for reimbursing Montreat College for any amount due.

Financial Aid Information

For financial aid information and application materials for the School of Adult and Graduate Studies (AGS), please contact the Office of Financial Aid:

Director of Financial Aid
Montreat College (MC 881)
P.O. Box 1267
Montreat, NC 28757
800-545-4656
agsfinancialaid@montreat.edu

General Information

The Office of Financial Aid is committed to providing financial resources to students who seek an education at an institution committed to integrating faith and learning. In partnership with college, federal, state, and other organizations, the Office will coordinate the administration of all students' financial assistance awarded to ensure equity and consistency in the delivery of funds to students.

Montreat College offers state and federal aid programs along with institutional discounts to assist students with funding their educational expenses. Each program offered has different eligibility requirements to qualify for the aid.

Types of Financial Aid

Students who are citizens or have permanent residence status in the United States are eligible to apply for financial assistance under various federal aid programs. Students must complete all the financial aid paperwork, including the Free Application for Federal Student Aid (FAFSA), to be considered for the following programs.

Federal Pell Grant
Pell Grant eligibility is based on the student's expected family contribution (EFC) from the FAFSA and their hours of enrollment each semester. Pell Grants are available only to undergraduate students. If a student drops a course included in the financial aid award or they are considering withdrawing from a course, they should contact the Financial Aid Office immediately.

William D. Ford Federal Direct Student Loan Program
Federal Direct Loans (subsidized and unsubsidized) are low-interest loans available to assist eligible students. A student must complete an online Entrance Counseling Interview and Master Promissory Note to receive federal loan funds. Upon meeting

all general eligibility requirements, the loan application must be certified by the College. A student must be enrolled and accepted as a degree seeking student in an eligible associate, bachelor or master program.

North Carolina Need-Based Scholarship (NCNBS)

Recipients must have been a North Carolina resident for the last 12 consecutive months, be registered at least three quarters time (9 hours) pursuing their first bachelor's degree, and meet financial aid eligibility requirements. Students must complete a FAFSA annually in order to know whether they qualify for this Scholarship. Funding levels are based on annual legislative action each year. For the 2014-2015 award year students enrolled for full time hours (12 credit hours or more) are eligible for $1,360 per year and $680 per year for students enrolled in ¾ time (9 credit hours) If a student withdraws from a class, fails a class, takes a leave of absence, or makes any other schedule change, he or she may not qualify for this grant. Students are eligible for the NCNBS funding in the Fall and Spring semester of each year. The funds will not disburse until students have matriculated into all their required credit hours. Typically this occurs in Session 3 but is dependent on the student's individual schedule for the Fall and Spring semesters.

Montreat College Alumni Discount

Alumni discounts are available to students who have graduated with a Montreat College Bachelor's degree or Associate's degree from Montreat Anderson College. A $1,000 credit will be applied to the tuition charges for the Graduate degree program during the first term and second term-$500 each term.

Employer Reimbursement

Many employers offer tuition reimbursement to employees in academic programs. Students should contact their employer for more information and notify the Financial Aid Office of any awards made. Most employers reimburse tuition after a course is completed, so it is advisable make arrangements to pay for several courses until reimbursement is made. The student is responsible for paying tuition and fees prior to starting a course. Students using employer vouchers should submit them by the course due date and pay any remaining balance by that date. If any employer reimbursement information changes, the student should complete the Information Change form and submit it to his or her advisor. The student's financial aid may be subject to change.

Veterans' Help Desk

The VA certifying official, located in the Office of Records and Registration, works with the Veterans Administration (VA) to assist in administering the education benefit programs to veterans or eligible relatives of veterans. The VA certifying official certifies enrollment, based on number of credits, length of courses, and type of courses (residential or distance learning), and transmits necessary credentials and information to the proper administrative office.

Before a student's enrollment can be certified, the VA certifying official will need the following:

- A copy of the Certificate of Eligibility for the student.
- Signed Memorandum of Understanding detailing the expectations for students using VA educational benefits. The memo has detailed information concerning status for each type of student.

A student must be admitted and actively enrolled in courses at Montreat College before enrollment verification for veterans benefits can begin. Students in the School of Arts and Sciences as well as the School of Adult and Graduate Studies may be eligible for the full monthly allowances, provided they are enrolled full-time as determined by the VA. Students are responsible for reporting any changes in enrollment or attendance to the VA certifying official as soon as possible.

To apply for VA educational benefits, go to https://www.ebenefits.va.gov/ebenefits/vonapp. To check on the status of benefits, contact the Veterans Administration helpdesk at 1-888-442-4551.

The VA helpdesk for Montreat College can be reached by email at va@montreat.edu or by calling 1-828-669-8012 x 3732. The *Memorandum of Understanding for Use of Education Benefits for Veteran Students* can be requested from the VA helpdesk.

Application for Financial Aid

Procedure

- Apply for admission to Montreat College.
- Request a FSA ID from the Department of Education at fsaid.ed.gov. Students must have this to complete their Free Application for Federal Student Aid (FAFSA).
- Complete the Free Application for Federal Student Aid (FAFSA) online at fafsa.ed.gov. It is advisable to file tax forms before completing the FAFSA, but it is not required. It is best to have the FAFSA submitted as early as possible.
- Financial aid decisions are made after a student has been offered admission. Students are notified via an official award letter via email.
- Students receiving a loan for the first time at Montreat College will need to complete the appropriate paperwork, including the Master Promissory Note and the Entrance Counseling Interview for William D. Ford Federal Direct Loans at www.studentloans.gov.
- Students eligible for educational benefits through the Veterans Administration or Vocational Rehabilitation should apply directly to these agencies and inform the Financial Aid Office of pending awards.
- Students must reapply each year for financial aid by completing the FAFSA.
- All outside scholarships or benefits (non-Montreat College) must be reported to the Financial Aid Office. Montreat College reserves the right to reduce institutional awards and/or federal loans due to outside resources.

If a student chooses financial aid as a method of meeting the financial obligations of the AGS program, students are encouraged to complete all financial aid paperwork prior to the start of their semester. If the financial aid paperwork is submitted after the second week of the semester, the student's financial aid award may be delayed.

All financial aid funds are posted directly to student accounts. They cannot be issued as a check directly to a student. Financial aid information and forms may be found at the College website: http://www.montreat.edu/admissions/tuition-aid/.

If a student is academically withdrawn from Montreat College from a course or due to non-attendance in a course, a portion or all of the federal and/or state funds may be returned to the Federal Government. If an outstanding balance remains on the student's account after this process has been completed, then it is the student's responsibility to pay in a timely manner any outstanding balance no longer covered by financial aid funds.

At the end of the federal award period, any credit remaining on the student's account from federal aid is sent automatically to the student regardless of the preference expressed on the authorization to retain funds.

Students who are interested in borrowing to finance their education should complete a Master Promissory Note (MPN) and Entrance Counseling for the William

D. Ford Federal Direct Loan through the Department of Education at
www.studentloans.gov.

Students eligible for educational benefits through the Veterans Administration or
Vocational Rehabilitation should apply directly to these agencies and inform the
Financial Aid Office of that benefit. Students must also report to the Financial Aid
Office any military payments, tuition assistance, scholarships, or employer tuition
reimbursement. Failure to report tuition assistance, scholarships, or employer
tuition reimbursement on the Admission/Financial Aid Application may lead to a
student's financial aid award being adjusted after being initially awarded, and the
student runs the risk of having her or his aid returned to the federal or state
government.

Bachelor and master students who are on active duty or retired military with a
current military ID card may be eligible for a 20% discount in tuition. This discount
may not be combined with any other discount. For more information, contact the
Student Accounts Office.

Note: Validation of all High School Diplomas
According to federal regulations, high school diplomas must be valid in order for a
student to be eligible for Title IV funding (i.e. federal funding).

Federal regulations require all colleges and universities to evaluate the validity of a
student's high school diploma if the institution or the Secretary of the Department of
Education has reason to believe that the diploma is not valid or was not obtained
from an entity that provides secondary school education (Higher Education Act §
668.16(p)).

Maintaining Financial Aid

To maintain financial aid, undergraduate students must remain in at least six credit
hours in order to be eligible for student loans. Graduate students should remain in
at least 3 credit hours in order to be eligible for student loans. Eligibility for the
Federal Pell Grant may also be affected by changes in enrollment. Students must
maintain satisfactory academic progress (refer to policy for details) and must reapply
each academic year for financial aid.

Students must maintain at least ½ time (6 credit hours for undergraduate; 3 credit
hours for graduate) in a given semester to maintain any in-school deferment. Any
periods of enrollment for <½ time can impact any existing student loan grace
periods.

Students who are in default on federal student loans will not be eligible for any financial aid until the default is cleared through the lenders and proof is submitted from the holder of the loans in question that the default has been cleared.

Note: Undergraduate students are considered to be full-time if they attempt at least 12 credit hours in a standard term. Graduate students attending a program in a standard term structure are considered to be full-time if they attempt at least 6 credit hours. Graduate students attending a program in a non-term structure are considered full-time if they are continuously enrolled.

Academic Year Definition

To be considered full time, an undergraduate student should be enrolled in a minimum of 48 weeks (16 per semester) of instructional time and a minimum of 36 credit hours (12 per term) attempted. To be considered full time, a graduate student should be enrolled in a minimum of 48 weeks (16 per semester) of instructional time and 18 credit hours (6 per term) attempted.

Financial Aid and Satisfactory Academic Progress

It is very important to note that there are two types of Satisfactory Academic Progress (SAP) requirements. The first type is called Academic SAP and applies to **all** enrolled students. It is monitored by the Office of Records and Registration. The second type is called Financial Aid SAP and only applies to students receiving financial aid.

Federal regulations (Sections 668.16, .668.32 and 668.34) require that schools monitor the academic progress of each applicant for federal financial assistance and that the school certify that the applicant is making satisfactory academic progress toward earning their degree.

At Montreat College, this determination of progress is made at the end of each semester, including the summer term, and before the financial aid office disburses any federal aid funds for the subsequent semester. To be eligible to receive Title IV federal funds, Pell Grants, SEOG, Federal College Work Study, Federal Perkins Loans, Federal Direct Loans or state and institutional aid, students must maintain satisfactory progress.

Adult Undergraduate Satisfactory Academic Progress for Financial Aid Purposes:
Satisfactory Academic Progress (SAP) has three criteria and students must meet all three:

1. A Qualitative measure: All students must maintain a cumulative 2.0 GPA
2. A Quantitative measure: All student must earn 67% of all credits attempted
3. A Pace of Progression measure: All students must complete their program in 150% of the credit requirements. For example, a program which requires 120 credit hours for completion must be completed in 180 attempted credit hours (120 x 1.5 = 180). This is also called the Maximum Time Frame (MTF) criteria and is also a quantitative measure.

One additional SAP criteria students should be aware of, especially if they plan to double major, is: automatic completion. All students who have completed all credit requirements for any of their programs will be considered as having earned a degree for financial aid purposes even if they have not applied for graduation. These students will not qualify for any federal or state aid at the point of automatic completion.

Adult Graduate Student Satisfactory Academic Progress for Financial Aid Purposes:
Satisfactory Academic Progress (SAP) has three criteria and students must meet all three:

1. A Qualitative measure: All students must maintain a cumulative 3.0 GPA.
2. A Quantitative measure: All students must earn 75% of all credits attempted.
3. A Pace of Progression measure: All students must complete their program in 150% of the credit requirements. For example, a program which requires 120 credit hours for completion must be completed in 180 attempted credit hours (120 x 1.5 = 180). This is also called the Maximum Time Frame (MTF) criteria and is also a quantitative measure.

Failure to Meet Satisfactory Academics Progress

Financial Aid Warning: Students who fail to make SAP may continue to receive financial aid for one additional semester. No appeal is necessary for this student at this time.

Financial Aid Suspension: Students who fail to regain SAP at the end of a semester on Warning are not eligible to receive financial aid. A student on Suspension has the option to appeal to have their eligibility reinstated. If the student's appeal is denied, the student remains on Suspension and can only regain eligibility once they meet all three of the SAP criteria.

Financial Aid Probation: Students whose appeals have been approved are placed on Probation. The appeal approval will outline what the student needs to do to keep receiving financial aid. This may range from the student regaining eligibility at the end of the next period of enrollment to the student meeting specific criteria as identified in an Academic Plan.

Reinstatement of Aid

Aid may be reinstated on a probationary status by meeting the requirements for SAP or by an approved appeal. If aid is reinstated, a probationary status will remain in effect. A period of non-enrollment does not reinstate aid eligibility. A student returning after an extended period of non-enrollment must still submit a SAP appeal.

Appeals

Students who wish to appeal the suspension of financial aid eligibility based on mitigating circumstances (i.e., severe illness, death of a close family member, severe injury, or other traumatic experiences) may do so by submitting the SAP appeal form, a letter of appeal and supporting documentation to the Director of Financial Aid within **ten days** from the date of notification that aid has been canceled.

All appeals must:
1. Complete the enclosed SAP appeal form.
1. Include the student's statement which identifies the mitigating circumstances that led to SAP not being maintained. In the first appeal, since SAP is cumulative, the student must address all unearned coursework which appears on the Montreat College transcript.
2. Provide supporting documentation, such as statement from the doctor, death notice, etc.
3. Include the student's degree audit, which may be obtained from the Office of Records and Registration.
4. Include the student's Montreat College identification number, or Social Security number, current address, and communication information.

All initial and subsequent appeals and supporting documentation must be received within ten days of notice. The Financial Aid Advisory and Appeals Committee will not review incomplete or partial appeals. All documentation is retained by the Financial Aid Office for audit purposes.

The Director of Financial Aid will take the appeal to the Financial Aid Team and notify the student of the decision to reinstate or deny aid. If approved, conditions may apply. If the conditions are not satisfied, aid may be denied in a subsequent term. As described in federal regulations, **all decisions at this point are final.**

The Student Financial Aid Office will review no more than two appeals from a student during the course of study.

Effect of Incompletes, Withdrawals, Failures, and Repeats
All incompletes, withdrawals, failures, and repeats are included as attempts when determining SAP for financial aid. Depending on when a student withdraws in the semester, their aid may be recalculated. Students should consult a financial aid counselor before making any adjustments to their schedules as it may impact their awards.

Effect of Changing Major/Double Major
A change of academic major or the pursuit of a double major does not extend eligibility for financial aid. Students are still expected to complete their programs within 180 hours. A student may appeal if they fail to make SAP for this reason.

Effect of Credits by Transfer, Examination, Military, and Life Experience
Transfer credits that have been accepted and count towards the student's program of study will be used as attempts and completes and included in determining SAP. Academic credits received via examination, military, or life experience are counted as attempts and as earned credit.

Effect of Auditing Courses
Students do not earn any academic credits for audited courses. They do not count in the calculation of "attempted hours."

Return of Title IV Federal Student Aid

In the event a student withdraws from a course or the entire program, either through nonattendance or by administrative withdrawal, does not return to the next course after an approved leave of absence, or is not making satisfactory academic progress, the Financial Aid Office is required to process a withdrawal calculation.

All calculations are based on the last date of documented class attendance within the student's period of enrollment. A period of enrollment is one-half of the financial aid academic year. All awards that include federal Title IV aid will be subject to the federal return of Title IV funds calculation. All nonfederal funds are subject to the Montreat College refund calculation. The College has a fair and equitable refund policy as required under Section 668.22 (b) (1) of the federal regulations. The Montreat College refund calculation is equal to the federal calculation but takes into consideration only nonfederal forms of aid.

The federal return of Title IV funds calculation determines the percentage of the semester actually completed for which the assistance was awarded the student. This figure is used to determine the percentage of the aid the student earned for the period of enrollment. All unearned funds are returned to the proper agencies in the order prescribed by federal and state regulations. These regulations dictate that the College is obligated to apply refunds in the following order: Unsubsidized Direct Student Loan; Subsidized Direct Student Loan; Federal Direct PLUS loan; Federal Pell Grant; Federal Supplemental Educational Opportunity Grant; other Title IV, state, private, or institutional aid; the student. Students must pay any charges remaining on their account after funds are returned to the proper agencies.

Financial Aid Attendance/Scheduled Break Policy

Attendance is monitored for all students at Montreat College in order to determine their eligibility for financial aid. If a student remains absent for 45 days or more without the proper paperwork, the student must be withdrawn from the program. If a student is a financial aid recipient, an R2T4 will be processed and federal and state funds may be returned.

Financial Policy Appeals

Any student who wishes to appeal a financial aid or student accounts decision must do so in writing to the Vice President for Finance at the following address:

Director of Financial Aid
Montreat College
P.O. Box 1267
Montreat, NC 28757

General Student Information
Standards of Conduct

The trustees, administration, staff, faculty, and students seek to be motivated by Christ's love for us, and we desire to reflect that love for one another; therefore, we are called upon to practice consideration, fair play, and concern in our daily interaction with each other as an expression of our commitment to be a community under the lordship of Jesus Christ. Kindness and consideration demand the deliberate consciousness of other people's feelings and an effort neither to hurt nor offend other members of the community.

Such high aspirations require an understanding of what Christian standards are both in and out of the classroom, and they can be reached only when each one in the Montreat College community makes an honest effort to incorporate them into the pattern of daily living.

An obligation for patience and for the effort toward redemption is inherent in a Christian community. At the same time, the College reserves the authority to ask those members to withdraw who do not accept its delineation of Christian standards, and who are unable to learn to live happily in the framework of ideals. Those who act or speak in an abusive or threatening manner will be shown zero tolerance.

Montreat College Student Email Accounts

Each student is assigned an email account prior to the first course. This will allow students to communicate with and receive communications from various offices attached to Montreat College such as Academic Advising, Records and Registration, Student Accounts, and Financial Aid concerning non-public information. Students may also communicate with professors who may not have a permanent office on campus. It is essential that all passwords for email and online access be kept confidential. No one from Montreat College will ever ask you for this information. If you have difficulty accessing your information online, contact Information Technology helpdesk at extension 3661. All students are required to check their Montreat College email on a regular basis. **Not checking the student email assigned by Montreat College is not a defense for not knowing vital information sent to students.** Should a student use an email that is not assigned by Montreat College requesting information Montreat College deems private, that information will be sent to the Montreat College email address **only** or to the home address via the postal service.

Change of Personal Information

It is the student's responsibility to notify the College immediately in the event of a change of employment, address, telephone number, email address, name or, any tuition assistance. Students must submit a Student Information Change form to their assigned academic advisors. The form may be obtained at www.montreat.edu/registrar-office/forms or from the advisor. Note that name changes must be accompanied by a copy of the new social security card and legal document associated with the name change.

Disability Services

The College will provide reasonable accommodations for known disabilities whether visual, hearing, mobility, medical, learning, or for other qualified applicants and students. Eligible students should follow these steps:

- Identify himself/herself to the Academic Advisor.
- Submit current documentation of his/her disability to the Academic Advisor.
- Be willing to participate in additional evaluation to confirm the disability, if requested.
- Provide clear recommendations for accommodations from a professional care provider.
- Request in writing the specific accommodations needed to enable his/her academic access.

The Office of Academic Advising and Student Services, in conjunction with Student Health Services, will assess a student's documentation and determine the reasonableness of the requested accommodations. This group of personnel serves as a liaison between students and faculty/staff, working individually with students to develop and implement a plan for academic accessibility.

Alcohol Policy

It is the policy of Montreat College that alcoholic beverages and their use is not permitted on property owned or leased by the College.

Smoke and Tobacco Free Campus Policy

Montreat College is committed to providing students, employees, and guests with a safe and healthy environment. Therefore, the College is a smoke and tobacco-free campus.

For purposes of this policy, "smoking" includes, but is not limited to, the burning (or simulating the burning), lighting, or openly carrying of any type of tobacco, tobacco-derived, or vapor products including, but not limited to, traditional and electronic cigarettes, cigars, cigarillos, and pipes, as well as the use of chewing tobacco and snuff.

It is the policy of Montreat College that smoking is not permitted anywhere on College property, whether owned or leased by the College. For purposes of this policy, College property includes any property owned by the College, leased by or in possession and control of the College, and any property owned by the College and leased to other entities for short- or long-term use. It also includes the Montreat Presbyterian Church (EPC) building and property.

Information on smoking cessation classes and educational efforts in the community is available to students and employees of the College. A resource area is located in the Health Center on the lower level of Bell Library.

Enforcing compliance of the Smoke and Tobacco-Free Policy is the responsibility of the campus community at large. College administrators, faculty and staff are asked to remind everyone of the Smoke and Tobacco-Free Policy and report violations to the Dean of Students. Campus police officers will also report policy violations.

The first time a student is observed smoking in violation of this Policy, a written warning of violation of the Smoke and Tobacco-Free Policy will be issued.

The second time a student is observed smoking in violation of this Policy, a $25 fine will be assessed and 10 hours of community service will be assigned.

A third violation will result in a $50 fine, 20 hours of community service and referral to the Dean of Students for consideration of further disciplinary action.

Visitors will be advised of this policy by way of campus signage and announcements prior to all community events such as summer conferences, athletic events, and concerts. Guests who fail to comply will be reminded of the College Smoke and Tobacco-Free Policy with a request that they comply in the future.

Policy violations by employees will be handled through the regular supervisory disciplinary process.

Policy on Non-Students in Class – AGS

Classroom meetings for the School of Adult and Graduate Studies are for faculty, faculty-invited guests, and enrolled students only. Students are not permitted to bring guests to class meetings. No exceptions may be made for children (including, but not limited to, children of instructors and of students) to remain in the classroom. Parents are responsible to make necessary provisions for their children to be cared for in a separate location than the classroom or Montreat College location. Students who bring children or other guests to class or the site location will be asked to leave and will receive an unexcused absence for that class.

Special Note: Leaving children unattended in a public area or site location, including empty classrooms, computer labs, lobbies, parking lots, etc. is prohibited. This policy does not apply to students with disabilities who have received written accommodations to be accompanied by a caregiver or academic support personnel.

Sexual Harassment Policy

Sexual harassment can occur in any academic context, such as a professor/student relationship, staff member/student relationship, student/student relationship, as well as within other professional employment environments, including practicum and/or internship environments.

Sexual harassment has been defined in the professor/student relationship as follows: unwelcome sexual advances, requests for sexual favors, and other verbal or physical conduct of a sexual nature constitute sexual harassment when grades or educational progress are made contingent upon submission to such conduct, or when the conduct has the purpose or effect of interfering with the individual's academic performance, or of creating an intimidating, hostile, or offensive educational environment. Romantic relationships should be avoided between a faculty member and student with whom the faculty member has a professional relationship.

The definition of sexual harassment in other academic and employment contexts is similar: Unwelcome sexual advances, requests for sexual favors, and other verbal or physical conduct of a sexual nature constitute sexual harassment when (1) submission to such conduct is made either explicitly or implicitly as a term or condition of an individual's employment; (2) submission to or rejection of such conduct by an individual is used as the basis for employment decisions affecting the individual; or (3) such conduct has the purpose or effect of unreasonably interfering with an individual's work performance or creating an intimidating, hostile, or offensive working environment.

The College will not tolerate sexual harassment or ignore complaints of harassment from students, staff, or colleagues.

For information specifically about sexual harassment and assault issues, including prevention & response protocols, please consult www.montreat.edu/safecommunity.

In order to report possible sexual harassment, contact AGS Administration at agsadministration@montreat.edu.

Academic Information

Academic Advising

All students are required to review an online orientation for their particular degree program and participate in a new student orientation and registration meeting with an academic advisor before starting any degree program.

Academic advisors make every attempt to give effective guidance to students in academic matters and refer students to those qualified to help them in other matters. However, **the final responsibility for meeting all academic requirements for a selected program rests with the student.** All students can arrange for an appointment with their academic advisor at any time during their degree program.

Course Registration and Scheduling Changes

Undergraduate: Advisors will create academic plans with students and typically enroll students in courses one year at a time. Students may adjust their schedules online via the course management system during the designated registration periods (see Academic Calendar). Advisors will then approve or decline the course selections of their advisees. Students will be eligible to register after outstanding obligations to the College have been met.

Graduate: Graduate students will be administratively registered for their entire degree program.

Credit will be awarded only for courses in which a student is officially enrolled.

Eligibility by course ID level: Courses numbered 100 and 200 are open to all undergraduate students; 300- and 400-level are open to juniors, and seniors. 500- and 600-level courses are reserved for graduate students.

Change of schedule: It is the student's responsibility to officially process all course changes through their Academic Advisor before the deadline as listed on the academic calendar. Appropriate signatures must accompany the schedule change form.

Adding a course:
- Students may add courses no later than the first week of the session for **on-ground** courses.
- Students may add courses no later than the Friday prior to the start of the session for **online** courses.

Dropping a course: The following Withdrawal Policy will be in effect for students:

- If a student withdraws from a course during the first week of the session, the course will be dropped with no notation on the academic record.
- If an undergraduate student withdraws from a course during the second week of the session, a grade of *W* will be recorded on the transcript. This shows as attempted hours but does not affect the GPA. Graduate* students enrolled in 8 week courses may withdraw through the fourth week of the session.
- If an undergraduate student withdraws after the second week of the session, a grade of *WF* will be recorded on the transcript which will impact the GPA as an *F* grade. Graduate* students will receive a grade of *WF* if withdrawing after the fourth week of the session.

*Graduate students on non-standard terms may drop a course prior to the first night of class without penalty, and may withdraw with a *W* after the first night of class and before the second night of class. After the second night of class, graduate students on non-standard term will received a grade of *WF* if withdrawing from a course.

NOTE: Please see the Student Accounts General Institutional Withdrawal Policy for information on financial implications when dropping a course.

Non-attendance policy: Students must attend the first night of each course or contact their instructors and advisors. If students miss the first night of a course, without contacting the instructors or advisors, the course will be dropped from the students' schedules. This could result in the reduction or cancellation of financial aid for these students. The students' schedules for future sessions will remain unchanged.

Students taking online courses must complete the course introduction forums or other assignments by 11:59pm of the first Wednesday of the course sessions. If these assignments are not completed, and the students have not contacted their instructors and advisors, the course will be dropped from the students' schedules. This could result in the reduction or cancellation of financial aid for these students. The students' schedules for future sessions will remain unchanged.

NOTE: If students attend a course or section for which they are not officially registered, they will not receive credit for the work.

Medical/Military Withdrawals: If students need to withdraw from a course due to extenuating circumstances after the last date to withdraw with a *W*, a *W* may still be granted. Such circumstances are limited to extreme medical conditions, military duty, or immediate family death/major illness. If this is the case, students should contact their advisor for the appropriate paperwork. They must also submit documentation to verify the reason for the withdrawal. These documents will be sent to the Director of Records and Registration for a final determination.

Maximum Loads: Undergraduate students are considered full-time when enrolled in at least 12 credits during a term. Students may enroll in 2 courses per session for a total of 18 credit hours in the term. One additional course may be added with permission of the Academic Advisor. Only students who have at least a 3.0 cumulative grade point average will be considered for an overload approval. New students are expected to take only GE 250 during their first session with the College.

> NOTE: CMHC students who wish to take two courses during one eight-week session must submit the appropriate CMHC form to the CMHC Program Director or the Director of Academic Advising and Student Services requesting permission for the course overload, and may not take a course overload for more than two consecutive sessions. These students must have a 3.5 cumulative GPA or higher. (See CMHC program handbook for more information).

Repeating courses: A student may repeat a course in which a grade of less than *C* was received by: (1) re-taking the same course at Montreat College or (2) re-taking the course at an appropriate accredited institution. It is the student's responsibility to notify their Academic Advisor of courses to be repeated at another institution and to receive prior approval of the course to be repeated. Courses that are repeated at Montreat College for a higher grade will have the better of the two grades included in the academic GPA calculation. Courses that are authorized for repeat at another institution must be successfully completed with a grade of *C* or better. The transferred course will apply as credit only, and will not replace the previous grade in GPA calculations. *Financial aid may not be awarded for courses that are repeated.*

Auditing courses: A student who wishes to take a course for no credit (audit) may do so by receiving approval from the instructor of the course. A specific registration form must be signed by the instructor and student and returned to the Office of Records and Registration for processing. Instructors may set their own requirements for course participants.

Course by Arrangement: On occasion, students may need a course that is required in their program but is not offered in a given term. If it is essential to complete this course for graduation or remediation, students should request a Course by Arrangement (CBA) from their Academic Advisors. Enrollment in a course by arrangement requires the approval of the Academic Advisor, the Student Accounts Office, the Financial Aid Office, the AGS faculty director, and the Office of Records and Registration. The petition should be completed and signed by all parties and received in the Office of Records & Registration by the Monday preceding the first class meeting to receive consideration and allow for registration. An additional charge will be assessed to all students enrolled in a Course by Arrangement.

Transferring courses: A student who wishes to enroll in courses offered by another institution must complete the required form and receive approval by the Office of Records and Registration. Failure to follow this procedure may result in loss of transfer credit for these courses.

Class Attendance Policy

The Department of Education requires Montreat College faculty to adhere to a strict policy for class attendance to maintain Title IV funding. The AGS programs emphasize group interaction in the classroom as well as in study groups. If students are absent, they do not gain the benefit of learning from their peers, nor do they have the opportunity to contribute to other students' learning. Classes meet for a minimum of four hours per week of instruction, not including the time required to complete individual homework for each class. The instructor must turn in attendance records of class meetings each week through the course management system.

Attendance at every class meeting is expected. If students miss two class meetings, final grades can be lowered. Montreat College AGS allows one absence (total of four hours) from class without grade penalty. If a student misses a second class, the final grade can be lowered a letter grade at the discretion of the professor.

Instructors may have a stricter policy but they must clearly indicate any other specific consequences for absences in their course syllabus. If it is not indicated, it is assumed that the penalty will occur according to the policy above.

Note: Students formally enrolled at Montreat College, who, for any reason, have not attended classes within one academic year, must re-apply for admission. (See Readmission of Former Student Policy)

Credit Hours

Montreat College recognizes and adopts the following statements of "Credit Hour" as defined by both the Federal Definition (Federal Requirement 4.9) and SACS policy statement on "Credit Hour," and the associated "Guidelines for Flexibility in Interpretation" as outlined below.

Appropriate academic departments will regularly review the Montreat College curriculum and academic committees as needed to ensure compliance.

Definition of the Credit Hour: For purposes of the application of this policy and in accord with federal regulations, a credit hour is an amount of work represented in intended learning outcomes and verified by evidence of student achievement that is an institutionally established equivalency that reasonably approximates:

1. Not less than one hour of classroom or direct faculty instruction and a minimum of two hours out of class student work each week for

approximately fifteen weeks for one semester or trimester hour of credit, or ten to twelve weeks for one quarter hour of credit, or the equivalent amount of work over a different amount of time, or

2. At least an equivalent amount of work as required outlined in item 1 above for other academic activities as established by the institution including laboratory work, internships, practica, field experiences, studio work, and other academic work leading to the award of credit hours.

Guidelines for Flexibility in Interpretation:

- A credit hour is expected to be a reasonable approximation of a minimum amount of student work in a Carnegie unit in accordance with commonly accepted practice in higher education.
- The credit hour definition is a minimum standard that does not restrict an institution from setting a higher standard that requires more student work per credit hour.
- The definition does not dictate particular amounts of classroom time versus out-of-class student work.
- In determining the amount of work the institution's learning outcomes will entail, the institution may take into consideration alternative delivery methods, measurements of student work, academic calendars, disciplines, and degree levels.
- To the extent an institution believes that complying with the Federal definition of a credit hour would not be appropriate for academic and other institutional needs, it may adopt a separate measure for those purposes.
- Credits may be awarded on the basis of documentation of the amount of work a typical student is expected to complete within a specified amount of academically engaged time, or on the basis of documented student learning calibrated to that amount of academically engaged time for a typical student.

The intent of the above flexibility as provided by Federal guidance is to recognize the differences across institutions, fields of study, types of coursework, and delivery methods, while providing a consistent measure of student work for purposes of Federal programs.

Textbooks and Course Materials

Textbooks can be ordered easily and conveniently from MBS Direct, a virtual bookstore. Montreat College has its own bookstore site on the MBS Internet site (http://direct.mbsbooks.com/Montreat.htm). MBS Direct fills textbook orders within

24 hours and ships them according to the students' instructions. Students are given access information when they enroll.

Computer Requirement

All students are required to have access to a computer that meets the minimum specifications for all courses in the program. In addition, students will be required to have a notebook computer meeting these minimum specifications during class time for certain courses. Ask your Academic Advisor for the AGS Student Computer Policy for additional information.

Assignment Format and Standards

For most courses, papers, projects, and homework assignments are to be presented in the American Psychological Association (APA) style formatting. The Modern Language Association (MLA) style formatting may be required for English and humanities courses. Individual instructors may give other assignment specifications. It is the responsibility of students to give credit for words and/or ideas not their own.

Study Teams

The foundation of the AGS educational philosophy and practice is the recognition of the distinction between the younger college student and the student who has assumed the adult responsibilities of self-determination, financial independence, and professional development. The focus of the program encompasses two critical learning objectives: shared participant responsibility for self-directed learning and small group dynamics. Professional and personal growth requires that individuals develop the skills necessary to manage their own learning.

Study teams help to develop the interpersonal skills necessary for effective participation in groups. Study teams are designed to increase involvement, enthusiasm, and the pursuit of topics in the course and assignments to a more advanced level. Students value the benefits of small group work, noting that the process of working in a small group encourages critical skills, including group decision making, how to disagree without being destructive, the cultivation of new ideas, and how to include all members in a discussion. These groups may gather for in-class activities and outside of the classroom setting. Online students may also form virtual groups.

Academic Policies

Grade Changes

All grades are final three months after the date of issuance. Grades will be changed due to a computational error within six weeks of the due date for final grade submission. Under no circumstances will a student be allowed to do makeup work to improve a grade once final grades have been submitted. All grade changes must be approved by the Director of Records and Registration.

Petitions for Exceptions

To petition for an exception to academic policy, students must submit a written petition, stating the grounds for the request and providing any supporting evidence. Petitions for exceptions to academic policies are to be submitted to the Director of Academic Advising and Student Services who will render a judgment or will forward the petition to the appropriate College office.

Academic Integrity Policy

Definition of Academic Dishonesty
Academic dishonesty, such as cheating on tests and plagiarizing on essays, violates the fundamental trust underlying all academic work—that the work be the product of the student who submitted it. Montreat College defines academic dishonesty as the representation of another's words, ideas, or images as one's own. It applies equally to intentional and unintentional quotations, paraphrases, visual images, auditory images, and all electronic means of storage and communication. When academic dishonesty occurs, these procedures will be followed.

Discipline of Academic Dishonesty
When an instructor suspects a student of academic dishonesty, the instructor will meet with the student to discuss the incident and determine, to the instructor's satisfaction, whether or not academic dishonesty has occurred. If, in the instructor's judgment, such a violation of academic integrity has occurred, he or she will present the charges, in writing, to the student.

The only possible disciplinary actions are a zero for the assignment or an F for the course. The student may choose to admit her or his guilt of academic dishonesty and waive a hearing. This involves signing the academic dishonesty notice that outlines the disciplinary action. The academic dishonesty notice will be retained in the student's academic record.

A student who does not agree to the instructor's charges must appear before a panel of three faculty members, appointed by the Vice President and Dean of Adult and Graduate Studies or designee, on charges of academic dishonesty. During the intervening period, the student must continue to attend class. The panel will convene a hearing with the student and the instructor at which time the instructor will explain the student's alleged violation. The student may choose to counter with evidence of her or his innocence or may admit guilt.

Punishment of Academic Dishonesty

If the panel indicates, by simple majority vote, that the student has been dishonest, the panel shall uphold the penalty assessed by the instructor. The Vice President and Dean of Adult and Graduate Studies will notify the student, instructor, advisor, and Director of Records and Registration, in writing, of the panel's decision. If the student received a failing grade for the course, the student may remove the impact of the F on her or his grade point average by successfully retaking the course. Two incidents of academic dishonesty will result in a student being dismissed from the College. The student will not be eligible to reapply to Montreat College for at least two years after dismissal. If the panel finds the student not guilty of academic dishonesty, it will notify both the student and the instructor.

If the student wishes to drop the course but has been found guilty of academic dishonesty, the student may withdraw with a grade of *W* or *WF*, according to the withdrawal dates on the academic calendar. The academic dishonesty notice will be kept on file if the student has admitted or been found guilty of academic dishonesty.

A student may be dismissed from the College without refund of tuition or fees after the second incident of academic dishonesty occurs (including, but not limited to, cheating and plagiarism). That student will not be eligible to reapply to the College for at least two years after the dismissal, and any readmission will be subject to review by the Vice President and Dean of Adult and Graduate Studies.

Exoneration of Academic Dishonesty

If exonerating evidence becomes available in the five business days following notification of the panel's decision, the student may appeal to the Vice President and Dean of Adult and Graduate Studies. Appeals will be heard only if they meet one of the following conditions: (a) discovery of new evidence or (b) violation of procedure. A student must remain in the course and work toward its successful completion during the appeal process. The student will be notified, in writing, of the final decision.

Academic Grievances

A student wishing to appeal an academic decision (including a course grade) which directly affects the student, should file an academic grievance no later than 15 business days from the date final grades were issued by the professor for the course in question. A formal grievance related to a grade may be filed only if one of the following conditions applies:

- The student can provide evidence that an assigned grade was based on arbitrary or non-academic criteria.
- The student can provide evidence that the criteria for evaluating the assignment or coursework were not applied or were misapplied such that the assigned grade does not accurately reflect her or his fulfillment of course requirements and/or course policies as stated in the syllabus (e.g., class attendance, grade standards, penalty for late or incomplete work) and/or other applicable requirements of the College.

Process for Filing an Academic Grievance

1. A student wishing to appeal an academic decision which directly affects the student should first present the issue to the faculty member or administrator making the decision. If a grade inaccuracy is determined, the instructor will submit a grade change request to the Office of Records and Registration.
2. If satisfaction is not reached, the student should present the issue in writing to the Vice President and Dean of Adult and Graduate Studies for review. Such a written grievance shall include statements of the grounds for the grievance, supporting evidence, and suggested steps to resolve the matter.
   After careful investigation, the Vice President and Dean of Adult and Graduate Studies may summarily dismiss the complaint if, in her or his discretion, the grounds for appeal are frivolous or do not otherwise rise to the level of a legitimate grievance. If the complaint is not dismissed, the Vice President and Dean of Adult and Graduate Studies will form a panel of two other uninvolved faculty members with whom he or she will review all applicable material and make a determination on the appeal. The panel may (a) recommend that the grade be changed, either higher or lower than the original grade, (b) recommend that the instructor revise course and/or grading requirements and reevaluate the grade accordingly, or (c) dismiss the case.
3. The Vice President and Dean of Adult and Graduate Studies shall inform the student of the outcome within ten (10) business days after the decision has been made. In the case that an appeal is approved, all official paperwork, including the student's grievance and the panel's decision, shall be sent to the Office of Records and Registration to become part of the student's academic record and to the Faculty Services office for the instructor's file.

Non-Academic Grievance Policy

A student wishing to appeal a decision made by the College which directly affects the student, but is not related to academic policy, should follow one of these procedures:

Informal Grievance Procedure

- Discuss the grievance with the Academic Advisor.
- If circumstances of the grievance prevent going to the Academic Advisor or if the Advisor does not resolve the grievance within 15 working days, the student may discuss the grievance with the Vice President and Dean of Adult and Graduate Studies. Upon counsel, recommendation, and approval of the Vice President and Dean of Adult and Graduate Studies, the aggrieved person may be advised to proceed directly to a formal grievance procedure.

The student may request a formal hearing by initiating the steps for a formal grievance.

Formal Grievance Procedure

Request: The student must file a written request for a formal grievance hearing with the Director of Academic Advising and Student Services. The request must include the specific grievance, a description of the incident(s) from which the grievance arises, and the relief being sought.

Committee: Upon review of the written grievance, the Director of Academic Advising and Student Services may ask for additional material and documentation. After these are provided, the Director of Academic Advising and Student Services calls a meeting of the Grievance Committee as soon as possible or within 15 working days of receiving the request. The Director of Academic Advising and Student Services serves as the chairperson of this committee whenever it acts as a formal grievance committee, unless the President directs otherwise. The Director of Academic Advising and Student Services, however, has no vote in the final decision of the committee.

Hearing: The committee hears the grievance together with such witnesses as it deems appropriate to the grievance and forwards its recommendations in writing to the Vice President and Dean of Adult and Graduate Studies within five working days of the close of the hearing. The hearing is closed and confidential.

Report: The Grievance Committee makes every reasonable attempt to reach its conclusion and make its recommendations to resolve the matter within 15 working days of the convening of the committee, and to present its report to the Vice

President and Dean of Adult and Graduate Studies for review and appropriate actions.

Appeal: The decision of the Grievance Committee may be appealed in writing to the Vice President and Dean of Adult and Graduate Studies by the aggrieved student or the Academic Advisor within three working days after receiving the decision. With regard to the informal and formal grievance proceedings, the decision of the Vice President and Dean of Adult and Graduate Studies is final.

Scope: These grievance procedures are in no way intended to limit the rights of students under applicable laws.

Retaliation Clause: No employee of the College may make any retaliatory action against any student of the College as a result of that person (1) seeking redress under these procedures, (2) cooperating in an investigation, or (3) otherwise legitimately participating in a proceeding under these procedures. Any violation will be regarded as a separate and distinct grievance matter under these procedures.

Undergraduate Good Academic Standing and Satisfactory Progress

Good Academic Standing and Satisfactory Progress

Degree-seeking students must maintain a cumulative GPA of 2.0 in order to maintain Satisfactory Academic Progress (SAP). A student who fails to maintain SAP is subject to academic probation or academic suspension.

Withdrawal from courses with a grade of *W* will not affect good standing or academic progress provided the student meets the SAP criteria of a 2.0 GPA.

Review of SAP will occur at the end of each regular academic term for all degree-seeking students enrolled in that term for any number of credits.

Academic Probation

Students whose cumulative grade point average fails to meet the criteria established for SAP will be placed on academic probation for the next semester. If at the end of that semester the cumulative average is still below the required minimum, the student will be placed on final academic probation for the following semester. If the necessary SAP criteria have not been achieved by the end of final probation, the student will face academic suspension.

Students on final academic probation will lose their financial aid. See Financial Aid section of Academic Catalog for financial aid implications.

If a student withdraws on academic probation, he/she will have additional requirements for readmission, as explained in the Admission Information.

Academic Suspension

The administration reserves the right to suspend a student from the College because of poor scholarship. Any student on academic or final probation who fails to meet the requirements of probation will be subject to academic suspension without refund of fees.

A student not permitted to continue for academic reasons may appeal the suspension in writing to the Vice President of Adult and Graduate Studies within two weeks of the suspension. A student who is suspended for academic reasons may reapply to the College after one term (see Readmission of Former Students under the "Admission Information" section *and* the Repeating Courses policy under the "Academic Information" section). If readmitted, the student will be placed on final academic probation.

Academic Second Chance (ASC)

An undergraduate student may appeal for an Academic Second Chance (ASC) to request academic forgiveness for Montreat College courses. Forgiveness may apply to a single four-month period or a continuous consecutive series of periods within which a student earned grades lower than a *C*. If approved, those terms would be excluded when calculating the student's grade point average. No courses taken during the period approved for ASC would apply toward requirements for a degree.

A student who wishes to petition for academic forgiveness must meet the following criteria:
- The student must have been separated from all institutions of higher learning for a period of two (2) calendar years.
- The student must have re-entered Montreat College and earned at least 12 credit hours at Montreat College with a minimum GPA of 2.5 on those hours. He or she must be currently enrolled at Montreat College.

ASC terms remain a part of the student's record although the forgiven periods in their entirety will be excluded when calculating the GPA. The refigured GPA will be the official GPA of the College. A statement to that effect will be placed on the student's record.

Academic Second Chance may be granted only once and applies only to Montreat College credit. It is important to note that ASC may not be recognized by other institutions. A student may submit a letter of appeal including a description of her or his current action plan to achieve academic success to:

Director of Records and Registration
Montreat College – MC Box 896
P.O. Box 1267
Montreat, NC 28757
registrar@montreat.edu

Graduate Student Good Academic Standing and Satisfactory Progress

Satisfactory Academic Progress

Graduate students are expected to maintain a minimum cumulative grade point average of 3.00 throughout their program of study. Students receiving a grade lower than a B- may be subject to additional program-specific academic progress policies as referenced in the "Program Degree Requirements" section of the Academic Catalog. As such, students may also be subject to immediate suspension per departmental requirements.

Review of SAP will occur at the end of each regular academic term for all degree-seeking students enrolled in that term for any number of credits.

Academic Probation

Graduate students who earn a cumulative grade point average below 3.00 in course work taken for graduate credit will be placed on academic probation for the next term. If at the end of that term the cumulative grade point average is still below a 3.00, the student will face academic suspension.

Students who receive financial aid must make satisfactory academic progress to maintain eligibility for federal and/or state funds. Financial aid may or may not be available for students admitted on probation.

Academic Suspension

The administration reserves the right to suspend a student from the College because of poor scholarship. Any student on academic probation who fails to meet the requirements of probation will be subject to academic suspension without refund of fees.

Graduate students not permitted to continue for academic reasons may appeal the suspension in writing to the Vice President of Adult and Graduate Studies within two weeks of the suspension. Graduate students not permitted to continue for academic reasons may seek reapplication in writing through their academic program director.

NOTE: Each graduate program may have further specific requirements for continuation; these are outlined in program handbooks or maintained by the department.

The Family Educational Rights and Privacy Act (FERPA)

Student: Any person who either attends or has attended Montreat College

Educational Records: Any record (in print, handwriting, microfilm, computer, or other medium) that is maintained by a Montreat College staff or faculty member and is directly related to a student except:

- Sole possession records: Personal records kept by a college official if they are kept in the possession of the individual who made the records, and information contained in the record has never been revealed or made available to any other person except the maker's temporary substitute.
- An employment record of an individual whose employment is not contingent on the fact that he or she is a student, provided the record is used only in relation to the individual's employment.
- Records maintained by the Montreat College security department if the record is maintained solely for law enforcement purposes, is revealed only to law enforcement agencies of the same jurisdiction, and the department does not have access to the educational records maintained by Montreat College.
- Records maintained by the Health Services Office if the records are used only for treatment of a student and made available only to those persons providing the treatment.
- Alumni records that contain information about a student after he or she is no longer in attendance at Montreat College and the records do not relate to the person as a student.

Annual Student Notification

Policy: Students are notified of their FERPA rights and procedures for indicating their FERPA release preferences in the annual Montreat College catalog and via emails sent at the beginning of each term.

Procedure for Student Inspection/Review of Records

Students have the right to inspect and review their educational records upon request to the custodian of the record.

- If a student is requesting to see only one item from their educational record (i.e. an unofficial transcript), no written request or appointment is necessary. Access will be immediate, subject to the availability of the custodian.
- If a student is requesting to see more than one item from their educational record, a written request must be submitted to the records custodian that identifies the record(s) the student wishes to inspect. The custodian will arrange for the access and notify the student of the time and place where the records may be reviewed. By law, access must be provided within 45 days from the receipt of the request. When a record contains information about more than one student, the student may review only the records that relate to him/her.

Montreat College Right to Refuse Access Policy

Montreat College reserves the right to refuse to permit a student to inspect these records:

1. Any financial records of the parent that may be in the student's file.
2. Letters of recommendation for which the student has waived his/her right of access.
3. Admission records if the student's application was denied or the student chose not to attend Montreat College after making application.
4. Records excluded from FERPA's definition of educational records.

Montreat College Right to Refuse Provision of Copies Policy

Montreat College reserves the right to deny copies or transcripts or other records if:

1. The student lives within commuting distance of Montreat College.
2. The student has a delinquent account at Montreat College.
3. There is an unresolved disciplinary action against the student.

Schedule of Fees for Copies

The fee for copies of educational records is .10 per page, plus postage if applicable.

Disclosure of Educational Records Policy

Montreat College will disclose information from a student's educational record only with the written consent of the student, except in the following instances:

1. To school officials who have a legitimate educational interest in the records. **A school official is**:
   - A person employed by the College in an administrative, supervisory, academic, or support staff position.
   - A person elected to the Board of Trustees.
   - A person employed by or under contract to Montreat College to perform a special task, such as an attorney or auditor.

   Legitimate educational interest includes:
   - Performing a task that is specified in a position description or by a contract agreement.
   - Performing a task related to the student's education.
   - Performing a task related to the discipline of a student.
   - Providing a service or benefit relating to the student or student's family, such as health care, counseling, job placement, or financial aid
2. To certain officials of the U.S. Department of Education, the Comptroller General, and state and local educational authorities in connection with certain state or federally supported education programs.
3. To the National Student Clearinghouse for enrollment and degree verification purposes.
4. In connection with a student's request for or receipt of financial aid, as necessary to determine the eligibility, amount or conditions of the financial aid, or to enforce the terms and conditions of the financial aid.
5. If required by a state law requiring disclosure that was adopted before November 19, 1974.
6. To organizations conducting certain studies for or on behalf of Montreat College.
7. To accrediting organizations to carry out their functions.
8. To comply with a judicial order or a lawfully issued subpoena (accompanied by a reasonable effort to notify the student).
9. To appropriate parties in a health or safety emergency.
10. Results of a disciplinary hearing to an alleged victim of a crime of violence.
11. Final results of a disciplinary hearing concerning a student who is an alleged perpetrator of a crime of violence and who is found to have committed a violation of the school's rules or policies.
12. Disclosure to the parent of a student under 21 if the institution determines that the student has committed a violation of its drug or alcohol policies.

Directory Information Policy

Montreat College designates the following items as directory information: Student's name, address, telephone number, e-mail address, date and place of birth, participation in officially recognized activities and sports, weight and height of members of athletic teams, dates of attendance, major fields of study, enrollment status, classification, expected graduation date, job title and dates of student work study, degrees and awards received, photographs, and the most recent previous educational institution attended by the student.

Procedure for Students Requesting to Amend Educational Records

Students have the right to request a correction of their educational records under FERPA. If a student believes the educational records relating to the student contain information that is inaccurate, misleading, or in violation of the student's rights of privacy, he/she may ask Montreat College to amend the record. The procedure for requesting a correction of the records is:

1. The student must submit a request to the custodian of the record to amend the record. The request should identify the portion(s) of the record the student wants changed and specify why the student believes that portion of the record to be inaccurate.
2. If Montreat College decides not to comply with the request, the student will be notified of the decision and also advised of his/her right to a hearing to challenge the decision not to amend the record.
3. Upon request, Montreat College will make arrangements for a hearing and notify the student as to the time and place of the hearing.
4. The hearing will be conducted by an individual who does not have a direct interest in the outcome of the hearing. The student will have an opportunity to present evidence relevant to the issues raised in the request to amend the record. The student may be assisted by an attorney of his/her own choice.
5. Montreat College will respond with a written decision within a reasonable period of time after the hearing. The decision will include a summary of the evidence and the reasons for the decision.
6. If Montreat College decides that the information contested is not inaccurate, misleading, or in violation of the student's right to privacy or other rights, it will notify the student, in writing, that they have a right to place a statement in the record commenting on the contested information in the record or stating why he/she disagrees with the outcome of the hearing.
7. That statement will be maintained as part of the student's educational record as long as the contested portion is maintained. If Montreat College discloses the contested portion of the record, it must also disclose the student's statement.
8. If Montreat College decides that the information contested is inaccurate, misleading, or a violation of the student's right to privacy or other rights, it will amend the record accordingly and notify the student, in writing, that the record has been amended.

Writing Center

Students are encouraged to take advantage of the resources provided by the Writing Center, located on the first floor of Bell Library at Montreat College's main campus (Montreat, NC) and also available on the Web (www.montreat.edu/writing). Student writing consultants are trained to assist students in developing strategies for specific college papers and in shaping strong written arguments. They also aid students in mastering grammar and punctuation, understanding research techniques, and in tackling related writing tasks. Writing consultants are available throughout the traditional academic year (summer excluded); electronic and phone consultations are also available (see the website for more information).

Program Evaluation

In addition to the ongoing course-by-course student evaluations, graduates will be asked to evaluate the Montreat College program via exit interviews, exams, and follow-up evaluations done at three-year intervals. Employers are also asked to participate in this evaluation. Information obtained from these evaluations helps the administration, staff, and faculty make decisions about modifications in the program.

Grading System

The academic proficiency of a student is indicated by the following letter system:

Grade and Associated Quality Points	
Grade	**Quality Points**
A	4.00 quality points awarded per credit hour
A-	3.66 quality points awarded per credit hour
B+	3.33 quality points awarded per credit hour
B	3.00 quality points awarded per credit hour
B-	2.66 quality points awarded per credit hour **(see graduate satisfactory academic requirements)**
C+	2.33 quality points awarded per credit hour
C	2.00 quality points awarded per credit hour **(see competency and bachelor core requirements)**
C-	1.66 quality points awarded per credit hour
D+	1.33 quality points awarded per credit hour
D	1.00 quality points awarded per credit hour
D-	0.66 quality points awarded per credit hour
F	0.00 quality points awarded per credit hour
I	Indicates incomplete work and is given when some portion of the work is unfinished. An *I* is given only when there are circumstances beyond the control of the student such as serious illness that prevents the student from taking the final exam or completing a course requirement. An incomplete must be completed within six weeks after the end of the course, or the *I* grade will be converted to the grade the student earned before the course extension was granted.
P	**Pass**, equivalent to a minimum letter grade of C; credit hours for the course are deducted from the total hours needed for graduation with no impact on the grade point average.
W	Indicates withdrawal from a course with permission and within the time limits and according to the procedures established by the Office of Records and Registration.
WF	Indicates withdrawal after the last day to withdraw and receive a grade of *W*. Factors into the grade point average as an *F*.
AU	Indicates a course which has been audited and no credit earned.
NS	Indicates an unsuccessfully attempted course or competency, where no credit or competency has been earned. Does not affect GPA or quality points.
S	Indicates a satisfactory work (used for work that continues over more than one semester), where no credit or competency has been earned. Does not affect GPA or quality points.

Grade Point Average (GPA)

The grade point average is computed by dividing the total number of quality points earned by the total number of hours attempted, three (3) times in an academic year. Courses with a notation of *W* will not be counted as hours attempted in computing grade point average; grades of *F* and *WF* will be counted as hours attempted. No quality points are assigned for grades of *F, WF, W, I, S, NS, AU* or *P*. Cumulative grade point average is computed on all courses taken excluding courses in which a *P* grade has been received (refer to the following section for information on incomplete grades).

Instructors have one week to prepare grades and have them posted after a course ends.

Incomplete Grades

Policy: A grade of *I* (Incomplete) may be assigned only if the student made proper arrangements with the instructor prior to the end of the course and the student has extenuating circumstances beyond their control, such as serious illness, which prevents the student form taking the final exam or completing one course requirement. The instructor files a contract for an incomplete, to registrar@montreat.edu, at the time grades are submitted**. The student and the instructor sign this contract; however, if the student is only able to contact the instructor by phone, the instructor may indicate this and sign for both. If the student does not initiate this contract, the instructor will assign the grade that was earned at the end of the course.

Once the grade of *I* has been assigned, there is a maximum time limit of six weeks after the end of the course for completion of all outstanding requirements. If all the course requirements are not completed within the assigned time limit, the incomplete grade will be converted to the grade that was earned at the end of the class. A student cannot have more than one outstanding incomplete grade.

Procedure: Grades of incomplete are removed when the instructor assigning such a grade submits a letter grade designation for the complete work. In case of a student's failure to complete such work, the grade recorded will be that which was earned on the last day of the class.

IMPORTANT: This form must be submitted by the professor WHEN the course grades are submitted through *Self Service*.

**No incomplete contracts will be accepted without the expressed permission of the Director of Records and Registration or the Vice President of Adult and Graduate Studies.

Online Transcripts and Grade Reports

Grades are submitted in the online course management system by the instructor within one week of the end of the course. Students who are in good financial standing may view and print their online transcript and grades by logging into their online account. Students who are unable to view their grades online may request a copy of their current grades from the Office of Records and Registration. Grades are not mailed; however, students may request a certified copy of their grades, if needed. Transcripts will not be released online or in hard copy if the student is financially indebted to the College.

Requesting an Official Academic Transcript

The official record of the academic accomplishment of each student who enrolls is maintained by the Office of Records and Registration. All courses attempted, grades awarded, degrees conferred, and the major program of study, along with identifying personal data, are certified on the transcript. Montreat College is a member of the National Student Clearinghouse. All transcript requests are processed online via the Clearinghouse at http://www.mystudentcenter.org or by contacting them by phone at 703-742-4200. Transcripts will not be released if the student is financially indebted to the College.

Enrollment Verification

Students, for various reasons, may need official written proof that they are currently enrolled. Montreat College is a member of the National Student Clearinghouse, which acts as an agent for all verifications of student enrollment. Please visit the Clearinghouse online at http://www.mystudentcenter.org or contact them by phone at 703-742-4200 to obtain an official enrollment verification certificate at any time.

Degree Verification

Employers or background screening agencies may need proof that a student has earned a degree, but may not require an official transcript. Degree verifications can be obtained through the Clearinghouse online at http://www.mystudentcenter.org

Inclement Weather Cancellation Policy

The College will normally make a decision regarding class cancellation by 2:00pm. Students can learn if classes are canceled on a questionable evening by the following methods:

1. Calling the main campus switchboard at (828) 669-8011, option 3. The Asheville and Charlotte campus switchboards will also be updated
2. Visiting the Montreat College website home page
3. Checking the Montreat College student email for an e-blast from AGS Administration
4. Checking with local TV stations (To sign up for text message and/or email alerts from an individual news station, please visit the station's website for more information)

Arrangements for making up a missed class due to inclement weather will be determined by the instructor and the students with guidance from Faculty Services and the Director of Extended Education and Outreach or the applicable Campus Coordinator. Each course module provides provisions for possible online make-up assignments.

Graduation Information

Undergraduate Degree Requirements for Graduation

In order to graduate from Montreat College, degree-seeking students in the baccalaureate programs must fulfill the following requirements:

- Earn a minimum of 126 semester hours for a bachelor degree, or 60 semester hours for an associate degree.
- Complete the General Education Core requirements and meet all General Education Competency Requirements.
- Complete the program core curriculum, including the major and the major concentration, if applicable.
- Successfully complete at least 33 credit hours in courses at the 300-level and above.
- Fulfill residency requirement specific to degree level:
  - Bachelor degree: two semesters and the completion of 32 credit hours taken at Montreat College, including 18 credits in the major.
  - Associate degree: a minimum of 24 credit hours must be earned at Montreat College.
- Attain a minimum 2.0 grade point average and earn a grade of *C* or better, with no more than 2 grades* of *C-*, in courses counted toward the major, the concentration within a major, General Education Core classes required by the major, and pre-requisite courses**.
- Payment of all tuition and fees.
  *The allowance of 2 grades of *C-* does not apply to General Education Competency requirements.
  **Pre-requisite courses that are not part of the major requirements may receive a *C-* unless otherwise stated in the catalog.

Students are subject to the academic requirements stated in the catalog that was current when they first enrolled as students. A student who leaves the College and is later readmitted must meet the requirements current at the time of readmission.

Graduate Degree Requirements for Graduation

See degree requirements specific to your master's degree.

Graduation and Academic Honors

For graduation with honors from a baccalaureate program, students must earn a minimum of 60 credit hours at Montreat College and meet the following minimum cumulative grade point average requirements:

GPA	HONOR
3.50 – 3.69	Cum laude
3.70 – 3.84	Magna cum laude
3.85 – 4.00	Summa cum laude

Baccalaureate degree honors are recognized by wearing gold cords at Commencement.

Baccalaureate students with 45-59 hours at Montreat College and a minimum grade point average of 3.75 or higher may graduate *with distinction*.

Associate degree students who graduate with a minimum grade point average of 3.75 or higher and complete at least 45 hours at Montreat College may graduate *with honors* Associate degree honors are recognized by wearing gold and white cords at Commencement.

Valedictorian and Salutatorian are recognized among baccalaureate graduates with the two highest cumulative grade point averages having completed a minimum of 60 hours at Montreat College. If there is a tie in GPA, the student with the highest number of credit hours earned at Montreat College will break the tie. A valedictorian and salutatorian are chosen twice a year, once in December from among the combined August and December graduates and once in May from among the May graduates.

> **Note:** Students in graduate level programs are not eligible for graduation honors. Bachelor degree students are not eligible for graduation honors until they complete their final Montreat College course; at that time, honors will be posted on the transcript and diploma.

Scholarship Pin is awarded to graduates receiving the bachelor's degree who have fulfilled the requirements for Dean's List (3.50 – 3.89 GPA) or Distinguished Scholars' List (3.90 GPA or above) for six (6) consecutive periods as noted on the official academic transcript.

Pinnacle (bachelor degree) and Spire (associate degree) Honor Societies, national honor societies for adult students in nonresidential programs, grant recognition to students for scholastic success and community leadership. Undergraduate students must meet all the following requirements:

- Minimum GPA of 3.5
- At least 24 Montreat College credit hours
- A commitment to community service through meaningful and active participation in at least three community projects or organizations during their time spent at Montreat College.

Chi Sigma Iota is an international honor society that values academic and professional excellence in counseling. It promotes a strong professional identity through members (professional counselors, counselor educators, and students) who contribute to the realization of a healthy society by fostering wellness and human dignity. Chi Sigma Iota's mission is to promote scholarship, research, professionalism, leadership, advocacy, and excellence in counseling, and to recognize high attainment in the pursuit of academic and clinical excellence in the profession of counseling. Students must hold a 3.5 GPA or higher in order to be members.

Military cords: Montreat College wishes to recognize those who are veterans or active duty members in our U.S. Armed Services. These women and men will be given red, white, and blue honor cords to wear during their graduation commencement ceremonies.

Undergraduate Term Honors

Dean's List consists of those undergraduate degree-seeking students who during the previous term met all the following requirements:

- Received a grade point average of between 3.50 and 3.89 on academic work
- Took at least twelve credit hours of academic work
- Received no grade of *I, F, WF*
- Maintained a satisfactory citizenship record

Distinguished Scholars' List consists of those undergraduate degree-seeking students who during the previous term met all the following requirements:

- Received a grade point average of 3.90 or above on academic work
- Took at least twelve credit hours of academic work
- Received no grade of *I, F, WF*
- Maintained a satisfactory citizenship record

Graduation

Application for Graduation

All candidates for graduation must submit a formal application for graduation to the Office of Records and Registration by the appropriate graduation application deadline: March 1 (May 31st Conferral), June 1 (August 31st Conferral), or October 1 (December 31st Conferral). This application is found on our website www.montreat.edu/graduation. Applicants for graduation must complete all degree requirements, complete the exit procedures of the College, and be in good financial standing to be eligible to graduate. **External credits and exam scores are expected to be on file in the Office of Records and Registration by the 31st of the month of conferral. Students who apply and do not graduate may be required to submit a new application and fee for graduation**.

Petition to Walk in Commencement (May and December)

If a student has not finished his or her final requirement the day before the ceremony, a petition to participate in a commencement ceremony is available. To be eligible to petition, a student must meet all the following requirements:

- be within three credits or one requirement of completing all degree and exit requirements
- have plans to complete the credits or requirement prior to the end of the next conferral
- have fulfilled all other degree and exit requirements
- be in good financial standing

Completed petitions must be sent to:

Montreat College
Records and Registration – MC 896
P.O. Box 1267
Montreat, NC 28757
registrar@montreat.edu

Students approved to walk but who do not complete degree requirements prior to the next commencement are required to submit a new application and fee for graduation. All degree and exit requirements must be completed by the last day of the month of commencement for a student to be eligible to receive a degree during the conferral period. Students may participate in only one commencement ceremony per degree. **Bachelor's degree students are not eligible for honors until they complete their final Montreat College course; at that time, honors will be posted on the transcript and diploma.**

Montreat College Undergraduates Entering Graduate Study

A Montreat College undergraduate student enrolled in a bachelor degree program and nearing completion when admitted to a graduate program is admitted to the graduate school contingent upon successful completion of the bachelor's degree. As students cannot officially start a graduate program of study until after the completion and verification of all degree requirements for the bachelor degree, students who are considering the pursuit of a graduate degree should file an application for graduation early according to the previous schedule (see Application for Graduation).

Commencement

Two commencement ceremonies are held each academic year (in December and May) to honor graduates. Candidates who have been cleared to participate in Commencement exercises are encouraged to participate. Graduation and commencement information is available at http://www.montreat.edu/registrars-office/graduation/.

An additional conferral period is provided in August for those who complete requirements during the summer. Summer graduates are encouraged to participate in the commencement ceremony in December. Completed students' diplomas are mailed no later than one month after the degree conferral date. Diplomas will be held until exit counseling, financial obligations, and all other requirements have been completed.

Degree Conferral

Requirements

To qualify for graduation, students must complete all requirements for their degree by the deadline for their particular degree conferral.

For May Commencement: All requirements and all documentation for the degree must be received by the Office of Records and Registration at Montreat College by **May 31**, and all information relative to requests for Non-collegiate Credit Assessment (NCA) must be received by March 31. These deadlines include making up incomplete grades as well as having official transcripts received by the Office of Records and Registration if courses have been taken elsewhere.

For December Commencement: All documents must be received by the Office of Records and Registration by **December 31**, and all information relative to requests for NCA must be received by October 31.

For August graduation: All graduation requirements must be completed and received by the Office of Records and Registration by **August 31**, and all information relative to requests for NCA must be received by June 30. August graduates will be invited to participate in the commencement exercise in December.

Fees may be assessed by the Office of Records and Registration to reprint a diploma when degree conferral has been postponed. **Deadlines are strictly enforced**, and any student with incomplete graduation documentation by the deadline **must reapply for the next graduation date.**

Academic Programs

Curriculum

Montreat College School of Adult and Graduate Studies offers an Associate of Science, Bachelor of Business Administration, Bachelor of Science in Management, Bachelor of Science in Bible and Religion, Bachelor of Science in Psychology and Human Services, Master of Arts in Clinical Mental Health Counseling, Master of Business Administration, Master of Science in Environmental Education, and Master of Science in Management and Leadership degrees.

In the associate core courses, students complete general education course work in Bible, writing, humanities, social science, public speaking, mathematics, and science. These courses seek to develop the whole person and to prepare students for successful completion of the bachelor program.

The bachelor and master core courses embrace the development of the adult learner and provide exposure to human problems and personal values through a well-planned, sequenced curriculum which integrates within the curriculum increasingly advanced cognitive skills, awareness of self and others, values clarification, and social and interpersonal skills.

Academic Programs
Associate of Science
Business
General Studies
Bachelor of Business Administration
General Business
Human Resource Management
Marketing
Bachelor of Science in Bible and Religion
Preaching and Evangelism
Bachelor of Science in Management
Bachelor of Science in Psychology and Human Services
Master of Arts in Clinical Mental Health Counseling
Master of Business Administration
Master of Science in Environmental Education
Master of Science in Management and Leadership

Undergraduate Degree Requirements

General Education Core

The General Education Core is the hallmark of a liberal arts education. In this series of courses, students gain the broad base of knowledge that will serve as the foundation for further studies in major areas. In addition, students will develop an appreciation of how the various collegiate discipline areas work together to gain a fundamental understanding of the structure and function of world culture from a uniquely Christian perspective. Undergraduate students complete the General Education Core specific to their degree level (explained under associate and bachelor degree sections, respectively).

General Education Competencies

All undergraduate students must demonstrate competency in the following areas: mathematical computation, oral expression, reading, writing, and computer literacy. Competency in these areas may be demonstrated as follows:

Mathematical Computation Competency: The study of mathematics at Montreat College prepares students to serve God and neighbor by enhancing their abilities to think logically and solve various kinds of problems by analyzing and interpreting data. Competency may be demonstrated as follows:
- Minimum grade of *C* in Math 102 or above or equivalent, **OR**
- Passing a comprehensive math test covering material in any MT course (form available in the course module), 102 or above **OR**
- Appropriate CLEP or AP scores, or equivalent class from a regionally accredited institution.

Oral Expression Competency shows graduates demonstrated skill in oral communication. Specifically, students will give extemporaneous oral presentations that either inform or persuade. Competency will be achieved when students demonstrate in the context of oral presentations clarity of thought, originality of ideas, organizational techniques, appropriate diction, critical thinking, supporting strategies, and effective delivery. Competency may be demonstrated as follows:
- Minimum grade of *C* in CM 231 or EN 371, or the equivalent **OR**
- Appropriate DSST scores, or equivalent class from a regionally accredited institution.

Reading Competency may be demonstrated as follows:
- Grade of *C* or above in a literature course (EN 200-level or above, excluding writing courses), **OR**
- Appropriate CLEP or AP scores, or equivalent class from a regionally accredited institution.

Writing Competency may be demonstrated as follows:
- Grades of *C* or above in both EN 111 and 112 or the equivalent, **OR**
- Appropriate CLEP or AP scores with essay included, **OR**
- Equivalent classes from a regionally accredited institution, **OR**
- Accepted transfer credit for EN 112 when student tested out of the EN 111 equivalent at previous school (testing out does *not* include progressing to the EN 112 equivalent after making less than a grade of *C* in the EN 111 equivalent)

Computer Skills Competency: All students enrolled at Montreat College must demonstrate computer competency. Competency may be demonstrated by one of the following completed within the last ten (10) years:
- Completing CS 101 with a *C* or better, **OR**
- By earning a *C* or better on the computer competency exam (CS 102E). Those who pass the exam will earn three (3) credits recorded as a *P* on the academic transcript.
- Equivalent class from a regionally accredited institution.

Computer competency is understood to include the following skills:
- **Word Processing:** This includes basic formatting and layout skills, including footnotes and endnotes, headers and footers, and integrating pictures and graphs in the text.
- **Spreadsheet:** This includes organizing data, formatting, basic calculations, and developing charts and graphs.
- **Presentation:** This includes incorporating text graphs, pictures, and hyperlinks into a presentation.
- **Internet:** This includes conducting online research and identifying and evaluating credible web sites.
- **E-Learning:** This includes accessing an e-learning program, participating in a discussion group, and posting assignments.
- **E-Mail:** This includes sending and receiving e-mail, sending attachments, and receiving and accessing attachments.

Required Courses Must be taken until Successfully Completed

Montreat College has chosen to require these courses for several reasons. EN 111 and 112 ensure that our students possess the writing skills essential to all other college coursework. They also provide a proving ground for the level of scholastic effort required of our students.

All degree-seeking students must be enrolled in the courses below, unless they have received transfer, AP, or CLEP credit for them, until they are successfully completed:

First Term: EN 111 English Composition

Second Term: EN 112 English Composition

Students may withdraw* from these courses but must re-enroll in them the following term. Students who do not pass a required course will also be required to re-enroll in the course the following term. If these courses are not offered at the student's primary campus location, they may need to be taken in an online format. EN 111 and EN 112 must be completed with grades of *C* or better or these courses must be retaken the following term. Required courses must be taken until successfully completed.

*Students may only *drop* these courses during the drop-add week if they need to take a break from classes during that session; these courses may not be replaced by other classes.

Humanities Definition

The faculty at Montreat College defines the humanities as those academic disciplines that focus on the study of the human experience, including timeless stories, creative works, ideas, and concepts within various cultures through the ages. This study enables students to better understand their life and world and, from this broad perspective, to make better decisions for the good of self and society.

While natural and social sciences describe and explain phenomena in the natural realm and in human societies, the humanities focus on the *interpretation* of human experiences. Thus, the humanities do not include the *creation* of works of art or literature, but rather the critique and appreciation of such works. The disciplines comprising the study of humanities may include: history, philosophy, biblical studies, languages, literature, art, architecture, music, dance, theatre, and film.

Natural Science

Colossians 1 states: "For in Him [Jesus] all things were created...all things have been created through Him and for Him. He is before all things, and in Him all things hold together." The study of life and physical sciences helps to intensify a spirit of inquiry and wonder at God's glory, as revealed in what He has chosen to create, as well as an appreciation of the role of human beings as stewards of that creation.

Montreat College graduates must understand the scientific method and be able to apply scientific principles to interpret, discuss, and create scientific knowledge in ethical and responsible ways that benefit human cultures and natural environments. In order to be responsible workers, citizens, and consumers, students must expand their understanding of the connections among various natural systems and think through sustainability and other current environmental issues.

Associate of Science (AS) Degrees

The requirements for associate degrees at Montreat College are designed to provide breadth in the liberal arts general education. Students earning an associate of science degree from Montreat College will be equipped with foundational skills to integrate into their professional careers, and prepared to pursue junior and senior level study toward a bachelor degree.

Requirements for an Associate of Science Degree

√	Degree Component
___	Completion of the requirements for the AS in General Studies *or* Business (60 credits)
___	Completion of the General Education Competencies*
___	Completion of 60 credit hours with a minimum GPA of 2.0 (a minimum of 24 credit hours must be completed at Montreat College)

*See the bachelor degree General Education section for explanation of competencies and other Gen-Ed components.

Associate of Science in General Studies Requirements		
Curricula	**Applicable Courses**	**Hrs.**
Foundation Course	GE 250	3
Bible	BB 101 & BB 102	6
Computer*	CS 101 or CS 102E	3
English Writing*	EN 111 & EN 112	6
Literature*	EN literature 200-level or above (excludes writing)	3
History	Choose two: HS 111, HS 112, HS 211 (one must be world)	6
Humanities and Arts*** (two areas must be represented) Applied courses <u>not</u> included (i.e. photography, piano, writing, speech).	Choose two: Art: AR 211 Music: MS 202, MS203, MS204, MS205 Language: French or Spanish Worldviews: IS 202 Bible: BB 200+ level English/Literature: EN 200+ level (except writing)	6
Mathematics*	Choose two: MT 102 and above (MT 122 recommended if planning to pursue BBA or BPHS degree)	6
Natural Science	Choose two: AT 111, AT 112, ES 111, PC 111	6
Oral Expression*	CM 231	3
Social Science	Choose one: Psychology, Sociology, Human Development, History, Economics	3
General Electives	Choose ~9 credits (approximately 3 classes)	9
Physical Education**	PE 110 (if age was less than 24 at time of admission)	(2)
	Total General Education Hours:	**60**

*This course is a General Education Competency
**For those required to take PE 110 (less than 24 years old at time of acceptance), credit will be applied toward the General Studies curriculum or as additional elective credits.
*** Students are only required to take 2 humanities courses for the AS degree. Students who plan to continue to the bachelor level are encouraged to take 3 humanities courses since the bachelor Gen-Ed Core requires an additional course in humanities.

Associate of Science in Business Requirements

Curricula	Applicable Courses	Hrs.
Foundation Course	GE 250	3
Bible	BB 101 & BB 102	6
Computer*	CS 101 or CS 102E	3
English Writing*	EN 111 & EN 112	6
Literature*	EN literature 200-level or above (excludes writing)	3
History	Choose two: HS 111, HS 112, HS 211 (one must be world)	6
Humanities and Arts*** (two areas must be represented) Applied courses not included (i.e. photography, piano, writing, speech).	Choose two: Art: AR 211 Music: MS 202, MS 203, MS 204, MS 205 Language: French or Spanish Worldviews: IS 202 Bible: BB 200+ level English/Literature: EN 200+ level (except writing)	6
Mathematics*	Choose one: MT 102 and above (MT 122 recommended if planning to pursue BBA or BPHS degree)	3
Natural Science	Choose two: AT 111, AT 112, ES 111, PC 111	6
Oral Expression*	CM 231	3
Social Science	BS 103 Introduction to Economics	3
Business Core	BS 101 Introduction to Business	3
	BS 206 Principles of Accounting	3
	BS 209 Principles of Management	3
	BS 230 Principles of Marketing	3
Physical Education**	PE 110 (if age was less than 24 at time of admission)	(2)
	Total General Education Hours:	60

*This course is a General Education Competency
**For those required to take PE 110 (less than 24 years old at time of acceptance), credit will be applied toward the General Studies curriculum or as additional elective credits.
*** Students are only required to take 2 humanities courses for the AS degree. Students who plan to continue to the bachelor level are encouraged to take 3 humanities courses since the bachelor Gen-Ed Core requires an additional course in humanities.

These charts are reflective of the entire associate program and maximum credits for the entire degree. A minimum of 60 credits is required for the associate degree. A minimum of 24 credit hours must be completed at Montreat College.

If students take a full load each term, they should complete this program in two years.

Students wishing to complete an associate degree while pursuing a bachelor degree must have the two-year degree conferred at least one academic year prior to earning the four-year degree.

Bachelor Degrees

The General Education Core is the hallmark of a liberal arts education. In this series of courses, students gain the broad base of knowledge that will serve as the foundation for further studies in major areas. In addition, students will develop an appreciation of how the various collegiate discipline areas work together to gain a fundamental understanding of the structure and function of world culture from a uniquely Christian perspective.

The requirements for bachelor degrees at Montreat College are designed to provide breadth in the liberal arts general education. Students earning a bachelor degree from Montreat College will be equipped with theoretical and practical knowledge to integrate into the work environment, and prepared to pursue graduate level study.

Bachelor Degree General Education Core Requirements		
Curricular Component	**Applicable Courses**	**Hrs.**
Foundation course	GE 250	3
Bible	BB 101 and BB 102 (Old and New Testament)	6
Computer*	CS 101 or CS 102E	3
English Writing*	EN 111 & EN 112	6
Literature*	EN literature 200-level or above (excludes writing courses)	3
History	Choose two: HS 111, HS 112, HS 211 (One must be world civilization)	6
Humanities and Arts: Choose three; at least two areas must be represented. Applied courses not included (i.e. photography, piano, writing, speech).	Art: AR 211 Music: MS 202, MS203, MS204, MS205 Language: French or Spanish Worldviews: IS 202 Bible: BB 200+ level English/Literature: EN 200+ level, (except writing) **BSBR** – BB 201, BB 202 required	9
Mathematics*	**BBA/BSM/BSBR** – MT 102 or above **BPHS** – MT 122	3
Natural Science	Choose two: ES 111, PC 111, AT 111, AT 112	6
Oral Expression*	CM 231, EN 371, or PR 310	3
Social Science	**BBA/BSM/BSBR** – choose one: Psychology, Sociology, History, Economics	3
	BPHS – PY 201/202 & SC 204	6
Seminar of Faith and Life	IS 461	3
Physical Education**	PE 110 (if age was less than 24 at time of admission)	(2)
TOTAL General Education	**BBA/BSM/BSBR**	**54**
	BPHS	**57**

*This course is a General Education Competency

**For those required to take PE 110 (less than 24 years old at time of acceptance), credit will be applied toward General Electives.

Bachelor Degree Academic Requirements for Graduation

In order to graduate from Montreat College, degree-seeking students in the baccalaureate programs must fulfill the following requirements:

- Earn a minimum of 126 semester credit hours.

- Earn a minimum cumulative grade point average of 2.0.

- Complete the General Education Core requirements and meet all General Education Competency Requirements.

- Complete the bachelor core curriculum

- Attain a minimum 2.0 grade point average and earn a grade of "C" or better, with no more than 2 grades* of "C-", in courses counted toward the major, the concentration within a major, General Education Core classes required by the major, the minor field, and pre-requisite courses**.

  *The allowance of 2 grades of "C-" does not apply to General Education Competency requirements.

  **Pre-requisite courses that are not part of the major or minor requirements may receive a "C-" unless otherwise stated in the catalog.

Students are subject to the academic requirements stated in the catalog that was current when they first enrolled as students. A student who leaves the College and is later readmitted must meet the requirements current at the time of readmission.

Bachelor Degree Layout

All degree-seeking students in the baccalaureate programs will complete coursework in three general areas: 1) General Education Core and General Education Competencies; 2) Major Core and Concentration, if applicable; 3) General Electives, including Prerequisites and Bachelor of Science (B.S.) credit hours, if applicable. Requirements and descriptions for each educational component begin on the next page.

General Education Core & Competencies

Program	Total
Bachelor of Business Administration (BBA)	48
Bachelor of Science in Management (BSM)	48
Bachelor of Science in Psychology and Human Services (BPHS)	51
Bachelor of Science in Bible and Religion (BSBR)	48

Major Core

Program	Core	Concentration	Total
BBA	27	21	48
BSM	45	N/A	45
BPHS	45	N/A	45
BSBR	45	Included in core	45

Electives, including prerequisites & B.S. credit hours

Program	General Electives, including prerequisites	B.S. Hours	Total
BBA	30	N/A	30
BSM	21	12	33
BPHS	18	12	30
BSBR	21	12	33

Program Baccalaureate Degree Total for All Programs = <u>126</u> credit hours

If students take a full-time load each term, they should complete this program in four years.

Bachelor of Business Administration (BBA)

The Bachelor of Business Administration (BBA) provides a valuable balance of theory and practical experience, preparing students to work effectively in today's complex business environment. The program promotes immediate implementation of classroom theory to the work environment.

The Bachelor of Business Administration degree program offers four concentrations from which to choose: General Business, Human Resource Management, and Marketing.

Requirements for a BBA Degree

√	Degree Component
___	Completion of the Bachelor General Education Core (51* credits)
___	Completion of the General Education Competencies
___	Completion of the BBA prerequisites
___	Completion of the BBA Core (27 credits)
___	Completion of a BBA Concentration (21 credits)
___	Completion of required electives (~27 credits)
___	Completion of the Major Field Test
___	Completion of Individual Business Project (culminates in BS 471)
___	Completion of 126 credit hours (two terms and 32 credit hours must be completed at Montreat College)

*EN 371 in the major can fulfill the Gen-Ed oral competency requirement.

If students take a full-time load each term, they should complete this program in four years.

BBA Prerequisites

- BS 352 Financial Accounting and BS 452 Financial and Managerial Accounting require a prerequisite of a lower-level accounting course. This prerequisite must be met by successful completion of one of the following (minimum grade of *C*):
  - BS 206 Principles of Accounting
  - BS 208 A Random Walk through the Financial Maze
  - Equivalent accounting course from a regionally accredited college or university (official transcript showing proof must be submitted to the Office of Records and Registration)

  In addition to fulfilling the pre-requisite requirements, the above courses will earn three hours of required elective credit.

- CS 203 Information Systems Technology for Managers requires students to first meet computer competency. This prerequisite must be met by successful completion of one of the following (minimum grade of *C*) within the last ten (10) years:
  - CS 101 Computer Applications and Concepts
  - Equivalent introductory computer course from a regionally accredited college or university (official transcript showing proof must be submitted to the Office of Records and Registration)

  In addition to fulfilling the pre-requisite requirement, the above course will earn three hours of general education credit.

BBA Individual Project

BBA students will be expected to complete a business/service project or business plan as partial fulfillment of the requirements for the bachelor's degree. Students are assigned a project advisor who will guide them through the project.

The individual business/service project is a capstone, integrative, real world learning experience, requiring each student to solve a business problem, provide a support service to a client organization, or develop an entrepreneurial business plan. For the business/service project, students will identify a client organization, define the problem to be solved or the services to be provided, and establish the client's results. Students will submit a final project report and present their project in BS 471 *Individual Business Project* to demonstrate their achievement of the desired outcomes and their ability to apply the knowledge and skills acquired throughout the BBA degree program.

Bachelor of Business Administration Core

Course	Title	Hrs.	Wks.
BS 309	Business Ethics	3	5
BS 320	International Business	3	5
BS 351	Economics: Micro and Macro	3	6
BS 352	Financial Accounting Issues	3	6
BS 437	Marketing Management	3	5
BS 452	Managerial Accounting Issues	3	6
CS 203	Information Systems for Managers	3	5
EN 371	Managerial Communications	3	6
BS 471	Individual Business Project (Capstone)	3	5
TOTAL		**27**	**49**

In addition to the BBA Core, students must choose one of the following concentrations: General Business, Human Resource Management, or Marketing.

BBA General Business Concentration

The General Business concentration is designed to provide students with a well-rounded understanding of various aspects in the business environment.

Course	Title	Hrs.	Wks.
BS 350	Admin. Theory & Organizational Behavior	3	5
BS 311	Business Law	3	5
BS 314	Data Analysis for Business	3	6
BS 403	Leadership and Human Resource Mgt.	3	5
BS 422	Issues in Corporate Finance	3	5
BS 413	Production and Operations Management	3	5
BS 460	Strategic Management	3	6
TOTAL		**21**	**37**

Human Resource Management (HRM) Concentration

HRM helps students develop an understanding of the fundamentals of human resource management and its relevance in business. The concentration addresses the legal and ethical components of the decision making process involved in the human resources environment.

Montreat College's BBA/HRM degree has been acknowledged by the Society for Human Resource Management (SHRM) as being fully aligned with SHRM's HR Curriculum Guidebook and Templates. The HR Curriculum Guidebook and Templates were developed by SHRM to define the minimum HR content areas that should be studied by HR students at the undergraduate and graduate levels.

Course	Title	Hrs.	Wks.
BS 307	Organizational Behavior	3	5
BS 313	Employment Law	3	5
BS 304	Labor-Management Relations	3	5
BS 403	Leadership and Human Resource Mgt.	3	5
BS 310	Total Quality Management	3	5
BS 413	Production & Operations Mgmt.	3	5
BS 308	Servant Leadership	3	5
TOTAL		**21**	**35**

Marketing (MKT) Concentration

MKT prepares students for a career in all aspects of marketing; how to identify customer needs, how to communicate information about products and services to customers and potentials customers, where to market, and the pricing of products and services.

Course	Title	Hrs.	Wks.
BS 350	Admin. Theory & Organizational Behavior	3	5
BS 311	Business Law	3	5
BS 321	Advanced Principles of Marketing	3	5
BS 331	Sales Administration	3	5
BS 338	Marketing Research	3	5
BS 435	Consumer Behavior	3	5
BS 440	Integrated Marketing Communication	3	6
TOTAL		**21**	**36**

Bachelor of Science in Management (BSM)

The Bachelor of Science in Management (BSM) provides solid instruction in managerial and leadership principles and theory with a focus on developing the leadership competencies required in today's work environment, both private and public.

The BSM degree is comprehensive and does not require students to choose a concentration. However, students have the option of adding a concentration to their degree by completing the coursework required for one of the following BBA concentrations: Human Resource Management or Marketing.

Requirements for the BSM Degree

√	Degree Component
___	Completion of the Bachelor General Education Core (51* credits)
___	Completion of the General Education Competencies
___	Completion of the BSM prerequisites
___	Completion of the BSM Courses (42 credits)
___	Completion of the bachelor of science electives (12 credits)
___	Completion of required electives** (~21 credits)
___	Completion of Individual Business Project (culminates in BS 471)
___	Completion of 126 credit hours (two terms and 32 credit hours must be completed at Montreat College)

*EN 371 in the major can fulfill the Gen-Ed oral competency requirement.
**Optional: Students may choose (but are *not* required) to add a concentration by taking one of the following sets of courses defined in the BBA degree program: Human Resource Management or Marketing. These concentrations are in *addition to* the BSM courses and B.S. electives, but may be applied to General Electives.

If students take a full-time load each term, they should complete this program in four years.

BSM Prerequisites

- CS 203 Information Systems Technology for Managers requires students to first meet computer competency. This prerequisite must be met by successful completion of one of the following (minimum grade of *C*) within the last ten (10) years:
  - CS 101 Computer Applications and Concepts
  - Equivalent introductory computer course from a regionally accredited college or university (official transcript showing proof must be submitted to the Office of Records and Registration)

  In addition to fulfilling the pre-requisite requirement, the above course will earn three hours of general education credit.

12 Bachelor of Science Hours

Students pursuing a Bachelor of Science degree must complete an additional 12 hours beyond the General Education Core and major requirements in mathematics, science, business, computer, or other designated coursework as listed in the degree requirements for each program of study. This coursework may not be applied to the General Education Core, the major, or any major concentration requirements.

BSM Individual Project

BSM students will be expected to complete a business/service project or business plan as partial fulfillment of the requirements for the bachelor's degree. Students are assigned a project advisor who will guide them through the project.

The individual business/service project is a capstone, integrative, real world learning experience, requiring each student to solve a business problem, provide a support service to a client organization, or develop an entrepreneurial business plan. For the business/service project, students will identify a client organization, define the problem to be solved or the services to be provided, and establish the client's results. Students will submit a final project report and present their project in BS 471 *Individual Business Project* to demonstrate their achievement of the desired outcomes and their ability to apply the knowledge and skills acquired throughout the BSM degree program.

Bachelor of Science in Management Courses

Course	Title	Hrs.	Wks.
BS 308	Servant Leadership	3	5
BS 309	Business Ethics	3	5
BS 311	Business Law	3	5
BS 322	Marketing for Managers	3	5
BS 340	Management Concepts and Issues	3	5
BS 342	Markets and the Economic Environment	3	5
BS 350	Admin. Theory & Organizational Behavior	3	5
BS 355	Small Business Management	3	5
BS 356	Globalization & Intercultural Understand.	3	5
BS 403	Leadership and Human Resource Mgt.	3	5
BS 430	Organizational Strategic Planning	3	6
BS 471	Individual Business Project	3	5
CS 203	Info Systems Technology for Mgmt.	3	5
EN 371	Managerial Communications	3	6
TOTAL		**42**	**72**

See BBA degree for *optional* concentrations in Human Resource Management or Marketing. Concentration hours may be applied to General Elective credits.

Bachelor of Science in Psychology and Human Services (BPHS)

The Bachelor of Science in Psychology and Human Services (BSPHS) equips students with the knowledge, skills, and experience they need for working in social agencies, churches, and other settings, as well as preparing students to enter graduate programs in psychology, counseling, and social work. This curriculum will engage a course of study that focuses on psychological theories and research about human behavior and psychological processes with an emphasis on developing and implementing skills for helping individuals and families face the challenges of our present society.

Requirements for the BPHS Degree

√ Degree Component

____ Completion of the Bachelor General Education Core (57 credits)

____ MT 122, PY 201 and SC 204 are required in the Gen-Ed

____ Completion of the General Education Competencies

____ Completion of the BPHS prerequisites

____ Completion of the BPHS Courses (42 credits)

____ Completion of the bachelor of science electives (12 credits)

____ Completion of required electives (~15 credits)

____ Completion of the ACAT exam

____ Completion of 120 credit hours (two terms and 32 credit hours must be completed at Montreat College)

BPHS Prerequisite Courses

Most 300+ level Psychology (and PY/HU) classes require a prerequisite of introductory psychology, which must be met by successful completion of one of the following (minimum grade of C):

- o PY 201 Psychology Applied to Modern Life
- o PY 202 General Psychology
- o Equivalent introductory psychology course from a regionally accredited college or university (official transcript showing proof must be submitted to the Office of Records and Registration)

12 Bachelor of Science Credits

Students pursuing a Bachelor of Science degree must complete an additional 12 hours beyond the General Education Core and major requirements in mathematics, science, business, computer, or other designated coursework as listed in the degree requirements for each program of study. This coursework may not be applied to the General Education Core, the major, or any major concentration requirements. If students take a full-time load each term, they should complete this program in four years.

Bachelor of Science in Psychology and Human Services Courses

Course	Title	Hrs.	Wks.
IS 310	Pre-Internship	3	5
PY/HU 300	Child and Adolescent Development	3	5
PY/HU 305	Adult Development and Aging	3	5
PY 310	Research Methods	3	5
PY 314	Personality	3	5
PY/HU 315	Abnormal Psychology	3	5
PY 320	Social Psychology	3	5
PY/HU 412	Theories and Principles of Counseling	3	5
PY 416	Learning and Memory	3	5
PY/HU 441	Internship	3	10
PY 490	Senior Seminar	3	5
SC 205	Marriage and Family	3	5
SC 311	Social Welfare and Social Services	3	5
SC 414	Counseling Adolescents and Families	3	5
TOTAL		**42**	**75**

Bachelor of Science in Bible and Religion (BSBR) with a Concentration in Preaching and Evangelism

The Bible and Religion program of study prepares students to pursue graduate studies in a broad range of fields as well as to prepare them to work with children, youth, and families in a variety of organizations both in the United States and other cross-cultural contexts.

Montreat College provides a unique mentoring environment that facilitates interaction between students and faculty both in and outside the classroom context. The department's commitment to exploring the relationship between faith and learning, alongside the relevance of the Christian faith for all disciplines of study, provides learners with a rich liberal arts experience to prepare them for graduate study or a wide range of occupations. The departmental faculty challenges students academically, assisting them in wrestling with the spiritual and practical implications of the subject matter. The full-time faculty is complemented by part-time and adjunct faculty who share the College's and department's mission, providing specific expertise to enhance the educational experience.

Students who graduate with a degree in Bible and Religion are free to pursue a wide spectrum of career choices. Some students enter the ministry by continuing their education in seminary and /or seeking ordination by their denomination. Others build on the knowledge and skills they acquired from the Bible and Religion major by entering careers in education, law, criminal justice, psychology, and counseling. Regardless of what goals are chosen, a Bible and Religion major prepares one for a career and a lifestyle guided by religious faith.

Requirements for the BSBR Degree

√	Degree Component
___	Completion of the Bachelor General Education Core (51* credits)
___	BB 201 & BB 202 must be taken as two of the three Gen-Ed humanities classes
___	Completion of the General Education Competencies
___	Completion of the BSBR prerequisites
___	Completion of the BSBR (including Preaching & Evangelism) Courses (40 credits)
___	Completion of the bachelor of science electives (12 credits)
___	Completion of required electives (~21 credits)
___	Completion of 126 credit hours (two terms and 32 credit hours must be completed at Montreat College)

*PR 310 in the major can fulfill the Gen-Ed oral competency requirement.

Bible and Religion Prerequisite Courses

- Most 200+ level Bible classes require prerequisites of Old and/or New Testament, which must be met by successful completion of the following (minimum grade of *C*):
  - ○ BB 101 Survey of the Old Testament
  - ○ BB 102 Survey of the New Testament
  - ○ Equivalent introductory Old and New Testament classes from a regionally accredited college of university (official transcript showing proof must be submitted to the Office of Records and Registration)

- The 400-level Preaching (PR) classes must be taken in sequence.

12 Bachelor of Science Credits

Students pursuing a Bachelor of Science degree must complete an additional 12 hours beyond the General Education Core and major requirements in mathematics, science, business, computer, or other designated coursework as listed in the degree requirements for each program of study. This coursework may not be applied to the General Education Core, the major, or any major concentration requirements.

If students take a full-time load each term, they should complete this program in four years.

Bachelor of Science in Bible and Religion (BSBR) Courses with a Concentration in Preaching and Evangelism

Course	Title	Hrs.	Wks.
BB 201*	Old Testament Theology	(3)	(5)
BB 202*	New Testament Theology	(3)	(5)
BB 208	Gospels	3	5
BB 211	Christian Doctrine	3	5
BB 302	Romans	3	5
BB 305	Biblical Interpretation	3	5
HS 353	History of Christianity	3	5
PH 301	Ethics	3	5
PR 310	Biblical Preaching and Communication	3	5
PR 410	Preparing the Gospel	3	5
PR 420	Preaching the Gospel	3	5
PR 430	Prayer and the Holy Spirit	3	5
PR 491	Seminar on Ministry	1	1
YM 303	Discipleship and Lifestyle Evangelism	3	5
YM 380	Administrative Ministry and Organization	3	5
YM 401	Spiritual Formation and Faith Development	3	5
TOTAL		**40**	**66**

*BB 201 and BB 202 must be completed as part of the General Education humanities courses.

Master of Arts in Clinical Mental Health Counseling (MACMHC)

Mission of the Counseling Program

The mission of the Counseling Program is to train candidates in the fundamentals of human development, human behavior, and counseling within the context of both a secular and Christian worldview and to guide them in developing a personal philosophy of counseling and professional practice in a variety of settings. The counseling program provides a forum for candidates to engage in reflective practice as professionals and to become life-long learners, active global citizens, and advocates for social justice.

The Clinical Mental Health Counseling degree program at Montreat College is based on the 2009 CACREP Standards.

A total of 60 semester hours are required to include the following:

- Completion of a minimum of 51 credit hours of graduate work at Montreat College (up to 9 credit hours may be transferred from a regionally accredited institution)
- A cumulative grade point average of 3.0
- If at any time a student receives a grade below a *B-,* the student must meet with the program director
- Completion of graduate course work within five years of the date of admission into the MACMHC program
- Successful completion of clinical counseling internship hours
- Successfully passing the Counselor Preparation Comprehensive Exam (CPCE) prior to enrolling in CN 675
- Payment of all tuition and fees
- Approval of the faculty

If students take a full-time load each term, they should complete this program in 3.33 years or 10 terms.

Master of Arts in Clinical Mental Health Counseling Courses

Course	Title	Credit Hours	Weeks
CN 600	Professional Orientation to Counseling	3	8
CN 605	Ethics and Ethical Practice in Counseling	3	8
CN 610	Theories and Techniques in Counseling	3	8
CN 615	Counseling Skills	3	8
CN 620	Spirituality and Religion in Counseling	3	8
CN 625	Counseling Across the Lifespan	3	8
CN 630	Multicultural Counseling	3	8
CN 635	Mental Health Diagnosis and Treatment	3	8
CN 640	Career Counseling	3	8
CN 645	Assessment in Counseling	3	8
CN 650	Group Counseling	3	8
CN 655	Research Methods in Counseling	3	8
CN 660	Crisis Intervention/Crisis Counseling	3	8
CN 665	Substance Abuse Counseling	3	8
CN 670	Gender Issues in Counseling	3	8
CN 675	Counseling Practicum	3	10
CN 680	Counseling Internship I	6	14
CN 685	Counseling Internship II	6	14
TOTAL		**60**	**158**

Master of Business Administration Degree (MBA)

A total of 43 semester hours are required to include the following:
- Completion of all undergraduate prerequisites
- Completion of a minimum of 37 semester hours of graduate work at Montreat College (a maximum of 6 credit hours may be transferred from a regionally accredited institution)
- A cumulative grade point average of 3.0
- If at any time a student receives a grade lower than a B- OR has a cumulative GPA below 3.0 at the end of a term, the student will be placed on academic probation.
- If at any time a student receives a **second** grade below B- OR has a cumulative GPA below 3.0 at the end of a **second** term, the student will be suspended.
- Completion of graduate course work within five years of the date of admission into the MBA program
- Successful completion of a business consulting project
- Payment of all tuition and fees
- Approval of the faculty

If students take a full-time load each term, they should complete this program in 2.33 years or 7 terms.

Prerequisites for MBA:
- BS 545 requires a prerequisite of BS 351 Economics or the equivalent of micro and macroeconomics courses.
- BS 550 requires a prerequisite of BS 422 Finance or equivalent.
- BS 560 requires a prerequisite of MT 122 Statistics or equivalent.
- BS 570 requires a prerequisite of BS 352 Accounting or equivalent.

MBA CORE

	Course	Title	Hrs.	Wks.
Part 1	GE 510	Introduction to Graduate Studies	3	8
Part 1	ML 540	Marketing Strategies for Managers and Leaders	3	8
Part 1	BS 530	Ethics and Legal Environment	3	8
Part 2	BS 550	Financial Management	3	8
Part 2	BS 560	Quantitative Methods	3	8
Part 2	BS 565	International Business	3	8
Part 2	BS 570	Advanced Managerial Accounting	3	8
Part 2	BS 580	Strategic Planning and Research Analysis	3	8
TOTAL			24	64

General Business Concentration & Capstone

Course	Title	Hrs.	Wks.
CS 536	Analysis of MIS	4	8
ML 510	Organizational Behavior	3	8
BS 579	Current Issues and Implications	3	8
BS 555	Entrepreneurship and Small Business Management	3	8
BS 545	Current Economic Analysis	3	8
BS 590	Management Consulting	3	8
TOTAL Concentration		19	48
TOTAL for Degree		43	112

Master of Science in Environmental Education Degree (MSEE)

A total of 31-34 semester hours are required to include the following:

- Completion of 31-34 credit hours of course work while maintaining a cumulative 3.0 GPA. A student's final total of credit hours may vary based on thesis requirements and transfer credits. *(A student may graduate with 31 credits only if the student is a North Carolina state certified environmental educator or if they can show proof of completion of the University of Wisconsin Fundamentals in Environmental Education course pending faculty approval).*
- A grade of *P* on the thesis or capstone project completed during the last semester the student is enrolled in the program.
- If at any time a student receives a grade below a *B-*, the student must meet with the program director
- Completion of degree requirements within 3 years from the start of the program
- Payment of all tuition and fees

Approval of the faculty

Master of Science in Environmental Education (MSEE) Courses

Course	Title	Credits
EV 500	Fundamentals in Environmental Education	3
EV 505	Introduction to the MSEE Program	1
EV 506	Research Practicum	1
EV 510	Instructional Strategies in Environmental Education	3
EV 515	Earth Systems	3
EV 516	Science Seminar	1
EV 520	Research Methods	4
EV 525	Designing Environmental Education Experiences	2
EV 530	Environmental History and Philosophy	3
EV 535	Environmental Communications	3
EV 540*	Survey of Environmental Education Curriculum Resources	2
EV 545*	Environmental Issues Investigation and Action	1
EV 550	Thesis Proposal or Project Design	1
EV 555	Ecosystems	3
EV 560	Thesis/Project	3
EV 570**	Nonresident Thesis/Project (If needed)	0
TOTAL		**32-35**

*EV 540 and EV 545 will be waived for students who have been certified in Environmental Education through the state of NC.

**Enrollment in EV 570 (Non-resident Thesis; $500 course fee) may be repeated until students complete the thesis/project.

NOTE: EV 581 Directed Study (1–6 credits) may be added to coursework at discretion of student and advisor.

Following the cohort schedule, students should complete their coursework in 1.66 years or 5 terms. Thesis/Project work must be completed within 3 years of the start of the program.

Master of Science in Management and Leadership Degree

A total of 42 semester hours are required to include the following:
- Completion of a minimum of 36 semester hours of graduate work at Montreat College (a maximum of 6 credits may be transferred from a regionally accredited institution)
- A cumulative grade point average of 3.0
- If at any time a student receives a grade lower than a B- OR has a cumulative GPA below 3.0 at the end of a term, the student will be placed on academic probation.
- If at any time a student receives a **second** grade below B- OR has a cumulative GPA below 3.0 at the end of a **second** term, the student will be suspended.
- Completion of graduate course work within five years of the date of admission into the MSML program
- Successful completion of a business consulting project
- Payment of all tuition and fees
- Approval of the faculty

If students take a full-time load each term, they should complete this program in 2.33 years or 7 terms.

MSML CORE

	Course	Title	Hrs.	Wks.
Part 1	GE 510	Introduction to Graduate Studies	3	8
	ML 540	Marketing Strategies for Managers and Leaders	3	8
	BS 530 OR CJ 530	Ethics and Legal Environment (General Business & Cybersecurity)	3	8
		Situational Ethics and Legal Environment in Criminal Justice	3	8
Part 2	ML 504	Exploring Leadership & Personal Leadership Development (3)	3	8
	ML 515	Effective Communication, Negotiating and Conflict Resolution	3	8
	ML 524	Accounting and Finance Skills for Leadership	4	8
	ML 542	Strategic Planning	4	8
TOTAL			**23**	**56**

General Business Concentration & Capstone

Course	Title	Hrs.	Wks.
CS 536	Analysis of MIS	4	8
ML 510	Organizational Behavior	3	8
BS 579	Current Issues and Implications	3	8
ML 512	Human Capital Management	3	8
ML 505	Management Consulting Service Project	3	8
ML 585	Advanced Entrepreneurship and the Entrepreneurial Spirit	4	8
Total Concentration		**20**	**48**
TOTAL for Degree		**43**	**104**

MSML to MBA

Students who have earned a Master of Science degree in Management and Leadership at Montreat College have the option to complete an accelerated Master of Business Administration degree.

A total of 22 semester hours are required to include the following:
- A cumulative grade point average of 3.0
- Once a student starts the MBA courses if at any time a student receives a grade lower than a B- OR has a cumulative GPA below 3.0 at the end of a term, the student will be placed on academic probation.
- Once a student starts the MBA courses if at any time a student receives a **second** grade below B- OR has a cumulative GPA below 3.0 at the end of a **second** term, the student will be suspended.
- Completion of graduate course work within five years of the date of admission into the MBA program
- Successful completion of a business consulting project
- Payment of all tuition and fees
- Approval of the faculty

Prerequisites for MBA:
- BS 545 requires a prerequisite of BS 351 Economics or the equivalent of micro and macroeconomics courses.
- BS 550 requires a prerequisite of BS 422 Finance, ML 524, or the equivalent.
- BS 560 requires a prerequisite of MT 122 Statistics, BS 314, or equivalent.
- BS 570 requires a prerequisite of BS 352 Financial Accounting Issues or equivalent.

Master of Business Administration (MBA) Courses
(Secondary to MSML Courses)

Course	Title	Credit Hours	Weeks
CS 536**	Analysis of MIS	4	8
BS 545*	Current Economic Analysis	3	8
BS 550*	Financial Management Practices	3	8
BS 560*	Quantitative Methods in Business	3	8
BS 565	International Business and E-commerce	3	8
BS 570*	Advanced Managerial Accounting	3	8
BS 580	Strategic Planning and Research Analysis	3	8
BS 590	Management Consulting	3	8
TOTAL		25	64

*requires a prerequisite; see above ** not required if completed in MSML.

Course Descriptions for the School of Adult and Graduate Studies: Undergraduate

Course Numbering System and Abbreviations

The first digit of the course number generally indicates the level of the course, i.e. 100 = freshman, 200 = sophomore, 300 = junior, 400 = senior.

Courses numbered 100 and 200 are open to all students; 300-level courses are normally open to sophomores, juniors, and seniors; 400-level courses are open to juniors and seniors.

The following list of abbreviations is used for academic subjects:

AR	Art	**IS**	Interdisciplinary Studies
AT	Astronomy	**MT**	Mathematics
BB	Bible and Religion	**MS**	Music
BS	Business Administration	**PH**	Philosophy
CM	Communication	**PE**	Physical Education
CS	Computer Studies	**PC**	Physics
EN	English	**PR**	Preaching
ES	Environmental Studies	**PY**	Psychology
GE	General Education	**SC**	Sociology
HS	History	**SP**	Spanish
HD	Human Development	**YM**	Youth and Family Ministries

Not every course listed in the Catalog will be offered each year. The College publishes a listing of courses to be offered each semester.

ART (AR)

AR 211S   Introduction to Music and Art
A study of the elements and principles of classical and popular music and visual arts, including an examination of their parallels through historical periods. *Humanities credit.* (3 credits, 5 weeks)

ASTRONOMY (AT)

AT 111P   Astronomy I
A study of the appearance of the sky, the sun, the moon; the theory of solar system formation and the resolution of conflicts between science and the Bible. *Natural science credit.* (3 credits, 6 weeks)

AT 112P   Astronomy II
This course will explore the means by which we learn about stars and galaxies. Stellar and galactic life cycles and the origin and structure of the universe will be considered. *Natural science credit.* (3 credits, 6 weeks)

BIBLE (BB)

BB 101S   Survey of the Old Testament
This course introduces the student to the tools and background necessary for understanding, interpreting, and applying the Old Testament to contemporary life. Furthermore, the course prepares the student to discuss intelligently the factual material in the Old Testament and to make clear critical judgments regarding the validity of various interpretations of the Old Testament. (3 credits, 5 weeks)

BB 102S   Survey of the New Testament
An introduction to the tools and background necessary for understanding, interpreting, and applying the New Testament to contemporary life, designed to prepare students to intelligently discuss the factual material in the New Testament and to make clear critical judgments regarding the validity of various interpretations of the New Testament. (3 credits, 5 weeks)

BB 201S   Old Testament Theology
An in-depth study of Old Testament themes with a view to their relevance for Christian theology, worship, and ethics. These include: God's self-revelation, creation, covenant/kingdom, fall, law, worship, prophecy, and hope. The course will include an introduction to proper exegetical, hermeneutical, and theological methods. *Pre-requisite: BB 101S. Humanities credit for non-Bible majors.* (3 credits, 5 weeks)

BB 202S   New Testament Theology
This course introduces the major themes of New Testament theology and their specific relevance for Christian theology, worship, and ethics. These include: the Kingdom of God, justification, sanctification, Pauline theology, etc. *Pre-requisite: BB 102S. Humanities credit for non-Bible majors.* (3 credits, 5 weeks)

BB 208S   Gospels

A study of the broad outlines of the life of Jesus and the Gospel literature of the New Testament. The course will examine the distinguishing theological interests of the gospel accounts, drawing particular attention to the similarities and differences between the Synoptic Gospels and the Gospel of John. *Humanities credit for non-Bible majors.* (3 credits, 5 weeks)

BB 211S   Christian Doctrine

A basic study of the major doctrines of the Christian faith and their application to contemporary thought and life. Includes studies in revelation, authority, the existence and nature of God, the person and work of Christ, the Holy Spirit, the Church, man, and Christian ethics. *Pre-requisites: BB 101S & BB 102S. Humanities credit for non-Bible majors.* (3 credits, 5 weeks)

BB 302S   Romans

An intensive study of the letter and its setting in Paul's ministry. The course also treats the biblical theology developed in the letter. *Pre-requisite: BB 101S & BB 102S. Humanities credit for non-Bible majors.* (3 credits, 5 weeks)

BB 305S   Biblical Interpretation

A study of the history, problems and methods of biblical interpretation, including a study of biblical-theological themes of the Old and New Testaments. *(Offered alternate years.) Humanities credit for non-Bible majors.* (3 credits, 5 weeks)

BUSINESS (BS)

BS 101S   Introduction to Business

This course provides an overview of the fundamentals of business management. *Strongly recommended for all business degrees* (3 credits, 5 weeks)

BS 103S   Introduction to Economics

An introduction to the basic economic concepts of what, how, and for whom to produce scarcity and choice, opportunity cost, price mechanism, competition, monopoly, demand and supply, the concepts of laissez-faire, and government intervention. Also included are macroeconomic issues, such as economic systems, aggregate supply and demand, and international trade. *Social science credit.* (3 credits, 5 weeks)

BS 206S   Principles of Accounting

A study of basic theory and practice for services and mercantile businesses, including rewarding techniques, statement preparations, and simple financial analysis with a view toward understanding accounting concepts. (3 credits, 5 weeks)

BS 208P   A Random Walk Through the Financial Maze

This course is an overview of the rudimentary elements of financial, managerial, and cost accounting. It also covers the basics of corporate and personal finance with some emphasis on the ethics of financial management. Topics such as the double entry system, inventory management (FIFO, LIFO, etc.), analysis of financial statements, and personal and corporate money management among other things will be discussed. (3 credits, 6 weeks)

BS 209S   Principles of Management

An introduction to management structures, including planning, organizing, leading, and controlling. Management process in for-profit and not-for-profit organizations, both large and small, are examined. Special topics include globalization, quality, Competitiveness, teamwork, ethics, and entrepreneurship. (3 credits, 5 weeks)

BS 230S   Principles of Marketing

An introductory study of the marketing process, including the elements of the marketing mix, the product distribution structure, the price system, and promotional activities. The importance of customer orientation is stressed. (3 credits, 5 weeks)

BS 304S   Labor Relations

A study of the history and development of labor relations, structure of union organizations, and process of collective bargaining negotiations and contract administration. With declining union membership over the last ten years, special emphasis is placed on employee relations in nonunion organizations. Contemporary issues include public sector and international labor relations. (3 credits, 6 weeks)

BS 307S   Organizational Behavior

This course examines the development and maintenance of organizational effectiveness in terms of environmental effects, improving motivation, behavior modification, systems aspects, communications, structure, and the dynamics of problem solving, goal setting, team building, conflict resolution, and leadership. *Prerequisite: BS 209* (3 credits, 5 weeks)

BS 308S   Servant Leadership

This course studies the functional, moral, and spiritual aspects of leadership in organizations. Students gain an appreciation of the nature, strengths and weaknesses of servant leadership and become prepared to develop as a leader according to a personalized leadership plan. (3 credits, 5 weeks)

BS 309S   Business Ethics

This course examines business policies and practices as they relate to moral and ethical issues. It raises basic questions on moral reasoning and the morality of economic systems both in the United States of America and internationally. It also examines the impact of governmental regulations on corporate behavior and the ethical relationships between the corporation, its employees, and its customers. BBA/BSM only (3 credits, 5 weeks)

BS 310S   Total Quality Management

An overview of the philosophy and tools of total quality management beginning with a study of W. Edwards Deming's Theory of Profound Knowledge. Students will be actively involved in team-building exercises employing statistical tools and techniques for innovation while solving real-world productivity problems. *Prerequisites: BS 209 and MT 122* (3 credits, 5 weeks)

BS 311S   Business Law

This course examines, analyzes, and applies the nature, formation, and system of law in the United States to the modern business environment. (3 credits, 5 weeks)

BS 313S   Employment Law

This course provides a comprehensive analysis of federal and state laws as they affect the human resource function, including equal employment opportunity, wage/overtime payment, employment agreements, and other restrictions on management's rights. Emphasis is placed on applying employment laws to develop programs that enable organizations to be proactive in meeting both company and work force needs, with an eye to resolving workplace disputes, preventing litigation, and implementing and administering personnel policies and practices in compliance with applicable law. No prerequisite. (3 credits, 5 weeks)

BS 314S   Data Analysis for Business

This course is designed to educate the undergraduate business student in the ability to work with data and statistical ideas. Students acquire the ability to accurately describe data, to make reliable inferences from data, and to critically assess the reported results of a variety of statistical studies by using various statistical methods and tools to analyze data in diverse example applications. Statistical methods and tools utilized include graphical and numerical data description, sampling techniques, probability distributions, tests of hypotheses, and analysis of variance. Emphasis is placed on understanding the purpose of each procedure, how to perform the procedure using the software tools, and especially how to interpret and apply the results to organizational problems. (3 credits, 6 weeks)

BS 320S   International Business

A study of business as practiced in different nations and cultures examining the influence of difference in the political, competitive, economic, social, legal, and technological environments on the main business functions (marketing, production, and finance) and business effectiveness. Also discussed are problems of international financial instability and exchange rate volatility. Foreign currency hedging problems are examined and solved. (3 credits, 5 weeks)

BS 321S   Advanced Principles of Marketing

This course involves an integrated analysis of the role of marketing and explores marketing methods within the total organization, from the sole proprietorship to partnership to the corporation. Specific attention is given to the analysis of factors affecting consumer behavior, the identification of marketing variables, the marketing environment, and the development and use of marketing strategies. *Students who have completed BS 230 may proceed with advanced marketing courses and skip BS 321.* (3 credits, 6 weeks)

BS 322S   Marketing for Managers

This course covers the principles of marketing that need to be understood by managers in order to develop and utilize effective marketing practices. Concepts of the global economy, including major social, psychological, and political influences, will be explored and their marketing implications considered from a manager's perspective. (3 credits, 5 weeks)

BS 331S   Sales Administration

A course on the professional, ethical, needs-based, non-manipulative, low-pressure, consultative approach to sales. Theories of selling, communicating, time management, and the relationship of sales to marketing and promotion are covered. Ethical business issues are examined in simulated selling situations. *Prerequisite: BS 321.* (3 credits, 6 weeks)

BS 338S   Marketing Research

A study of the role of research in marketing decisions. Special emphasis is placed on data gathering, compilation, analysis, and interpretation including the writing and analysis of surveys. Students will work on business problems with actual companies or evaluate new product concepts. *Prerequisite: BS 321.* (3 credits, 5 weeks)

BS 340S   Management Concepts and Issues

This course explores what it means to be a manager: who a manager is, what a manager does, and what a manager is responsible for achieving. This course surveys major concepts and issues involving the interrelated functions of planning and control, organizing, and leadership in 21st-century organizations and, building on this background, challenges students to become better managers. Extensive use of self-assessments as well as descriptive presentations, experiential exercises and analytical case exercises involving group discussion, written examinations, and a group research project enable students to develop their understanding and ability to apply ethical principles of sound practice in the workplace. (3 credits, 5 weeks)

BS 342S   Markets and the Economic Environment

This course first introduces the student to the economic way of thinking, primarily by stressing the notion of cost-benefit analysis and its critical importance to sound decision making. The focus then shifts to a study of the economic environment within which a firm must make its operating and financing decisions. The bulk of the course, therefore, addresses traditional macroeconomic issues with an emphasis on the business cycle and on the nature and effects of monetary and fiscal policies. This study of the economic environment is then extended to the international realm through a discussion of foreign trade and exchange rates. Throughout, the course stresses an intuitive and applied approach to understanding economic relationships. (3 credits, 5 weeks)

BS 350S   Administrative Theory and Organizational Behavior

A study of management techniques and leadership and their application to improving managerial effectiveness. The course stresses the importance of wholesome relationships between persons in business and maintaining sound relationships among employer, employee, and customer. (3 credits, 5 weeks)

BS 351S   Economics: Theory, Concepts, and Ideas of Micro and Macro

A survey of microeconomic issues such as price, competition, monopoly, oligopoly, income distribution, international trade, and economic development. The course also includes a survey of macroeconomic issues such as the structure of modern economics, its production, interrelationships, the nature and function of money, monetary and fiscal policy, and public finance. (3 credits, 6 weeks)

BS 352S   Financial Accounting Issues

This course is a survey of accounting procedures, with emphasis on identifying, recording, classifying, and interpreting transactions and other events relating to proprietorships, partnerships, and corporations. *Prerequisite: BS 206 or BS 208* (3 credits, 6 weeks)

BS 355S   Small Business Management

This course covers the role of a small business manager as distinct from that of an entrepreneur or that of a large corporate manager. Issues such as human resource management, financial management, marketing and the impact of global business on small firms will be examined. (3 credits, 5 weeks)

BS 356S   Globalization and Intercultural Understanding

This course examines the role of managers in a global environment.
The impact of globalization, culture, and diversity on management styles and techniques will be discussed. (3 credits, 5 weeks)

BS 403S   Leadership and Human Resource Management

A study of the leadership, technical, and legal issues confronting human resource managers in today's dynamic business environment. Includes an examination of principles and techniques utilized to effectively lead and manage the human resource/personnel staff function in modern business organizations. *Recommended prerequisite: BS 350.* (3 credits, 5 weeks)

BS 413S   Production and Operations Management

A study of the management of production functions in manufacturing or service environments. Using software applications, students apply quantitative techniques to aid in solving a variety of business decision-making problems. Topics include inventory control, forecasting, decision theory, quality control, and project management. (3 credits, 5 weeks)

BS 422S   Issues in Corporate Finance

This course lays the groundwork for determining the value of the organization by conveying the ideas of cash flow, time value of money, bond and stock valuation, and capital budgeting. Pre-requisite: BS 352.
(3 credits, 5 weeks)

BS 430S   Organizational Strategic Planning

This course provides students with an overview of the strategic management process. Emphasis is placed on developing a vision, setting objectives, crafting a strategic plan, and implementation. The course also stresses the importance of analyzing external competitive conditions and the organization's internal capabilities, resources, strengths, and weaknesses in order to gain and sustain a competitive advantage. Approaches to organizational structure, policy, support systems, and leadership required to effectively execute strategy are all examined. Case studies of real world companies are utilized to reinforce the theoretical concepts learned in the course. *Taken after all courses in BSM program except BS 471* (3 credits, 6 weeks)

BS 435S   Consumer Behavior

This course stresses the understanding of consumer behavior in developing marketing strategy. Opportunities are provided for the analysis of advertising's objective, target audience, and the underlying behavioral assumptions. Students will apply consumer behavior knowledge to social and regulatory issues as well as to business and personal issues. *Prerequisite: BS 321.* (3 credits, 5 weeks)

BS 437S   Marketing Management

An integrated course in marketing systematically oriented with emphasis on the marketing mix and the formulation of competitive strategies. Special attention is given to the control function, market analysis, marketing information, and sales forecasting. Case analysis is stressed. (3 credits, 5 weeks)

BS 440S   Integrated Marketing

This course examines the formulation of integrated marketing communication strategies to achieve marketing objectives; examines the use of traditional and nontraditional media; and analyzes the use of advertising, sales promotions, public relations, sponsorships, and other communication resources to promote sales, position products, develop brand equity, and support marketing actions. (3 credits, 5 weeks)

BS 452S   Managerial Accounting Issues

This course is an in-depth study of the role that accounting data plays in the decision-making process of managers of both for-profit and nonprofit organizations. *Prerequisite: BS 352.* (3 credits, 6 weeks)

BS 460S   Strategic Management

This course is designed to provide an overview of the strategic management process. Emphasis is placed on developing vision, setting objectives, and crafting strategy to achieve desired results.

Also stressed is the importance of analyzing external competitive conditions and the organization's internal capabilities, resources, strengths, and weaknesses in order to gain and sustain a competitive advantage. Approaches to organizational structure, policy, support systems, and leadership required to effectively execute strategy are examined. (3 credits, 6 weeks) *Taken after all courses in BBA program except BS 471*

BS 471S   Individual Business Project

An integrative capstone real world learning experience requiring each student to solve a business problem and/or provide a support service to a client organization. Through a preliminary project proposal, the student identifies the enlisted client organization, defines the problem being solved and the services being provided, and establishes the client's desired result. Through a project report and presentation, the student demonstrates achievement of the desired results by application of knowledge and skills acquired throughout the degree program. In place of solving a business problem and/or providing a support service to a client organization, a student may prepare a business plan for an entrepreneurial business venture that he/she is interested in pursuing. *Prerequisite: Completion of all BBA or BSM core courses.* (3 credits, 5 weeks)

COMMUNICATION (CM)

CM 231S   Public Speaking and Presentations
Instruction is given in the oral communication of original ideas, with special emphasis on impromptu and extemporaneous speaking styles essential to success in the classroom and workplace. Students receive specific training in the organizational and thinking skills needed to structure informative and persuasive speeches, as well as the performance skills required to effect confident, authoritative presentations. *Oral expression competency.* (3 credits, 5 weeks)

COMPUTER STUDIES (CS)

CS 101S   Computer Applications and Concepts
An introduction to computer hardware and software, with an emphasis on basic applications and concepts. Basic competence with word processing, online learning, and Internet navigation and communication will be acquired. The course includes an introduction to spreadsheets and presentation software. *Computer usage competency.* (3 credits, 5 weeks)

CS 203S   Information Systems Technology for Managers
This course provides a thorough overview of information systems technology for management. Through lecture, case study, Internet exploration and hands-on applications, students examine a wide variety of critical uses of information technology by management. *Prerequisite: completed computer usage competency* (3 credits, 5 weeks)

CS 208P   Microsoft Excel Introductory
This course uses excel to create basic spreadsheet applications containing formulas with absolute and relative cell addressing, built-in functions, charts, and drawing objects. This course covers the following Excel skills: creating and editing worksheets containing data and formulas, managing workbooks and files, modifying worksheets through copy and paste, drag and drop, Auto fill, and inserting and deleting rows and columns, and formatting and printing worksheets to enhance worksheet appearance and customize print output. The course is conducted using a case-based, problem solving approach emphasizing the What, Why, and How of the above Excel application skills. *Prerequisite: completed computer usage competency.* (3 credits, 5 weeks)

CS 209P   Microsoft Excel Intermediate
This course covers the following skills: *using date & time, financial, and logical functions in decision-making applications; *organizing, manipulating and consolidating data in large worksheets and multiple worksheet applications; *creating, sorting, and filtering worksheet lists; *analyzing decision alternatives using Pivot Tables, data tables, goal seeking, solver and scenario manager; *using lookup and reference functions; *importing and exporting data; *developing workbook applications including workbook sharing, conditional formatting, data validation and macro automation. *Prerequisite: CS 208P or equivalent.* (3 credits, 5 weeks)

ENGLISH (EN)

EN 111S   **Writing and Research for Adults**

This course involves studying and practicing those matters of writing that affect readability, including effective style (accuracy, clarity, and conciseness), appropriate punctuation, and correct use of grammar. Students are instructed in prewriting, composing, and rewriting. *Meets ½ of writing competency.* (3 credits, 6 weeks)

EN 112S   **Writing and Literary Analysis**

This course emphasizes the interconnectedness of reading and writing and provides additional practice in the writing process developed in English 111, including collecting information and ideas (through observation, reading, and exchanging thoughts and opinions with others) and planning and developing essays (through drafting, peer exchange, and revision). In addition, students read, reflect, and report on literature in order to develop and deepen analytical and imaginative thinking, writing abilities, and research skills. *Meets ½ of writing competency. Prerequisite: EN 111* (3 credits, 5 weeks)

EN 211S   **Masterpieces of Literature**

Students read and discuss selections from world literature, focusing on themes such as the human relationship to nature, God, others, and self. This course emphasizes the way in which reading, discussing, and writing about literature are foundational to understanding the human condition. While the principles of the writing process as presented in EN 111 and 112 are built upon, writing assignments will require a close reading and analysis of selected plays, poems, and novels. *Prerequisite: EN 111 and EN 112 Reading competency* or *Humanities credit.* (3 credits, 5 weeks)

EN 251P   **The Christian World of C. S. Lewis**

A study of C. S. Lewis' important, imaginative, and analytical works reflecting his Christian world view. As one of the twentieth century's most prolific and influential Christian writers, Lewis' work is a treasure trove for those seeking to learn how to think deeply about Christianity. His clear, lucid writing is especially helpful when he addresses complex issues, and his use of illustrations by way of analogy frequently sheds light on previously dark and thorny issues. Students will read and discuss his popular works focusing on his Christian worldview, write a series of short essays in which they engage Lewis' ideas and evaluate their merits and work together to present a final group research project. *Prerequisite: EN 111 and EN 112. Reading competency* or *Humanities credit.* (3 credits, 5 weeks)

EN 252P   **Shakespeare: Models in Leadership**

This course is a study of leadership as reflected in the works of William Shakespeare. This course will explore various models of leadership as illustrated in several of Shakespeare's plays with an eye toward applying his insights to contemporary business environments. *Prerequisite: EN 111 and EN 112. Reading competency* or *Humanities credit.* (3 credits, 5 weeks)

EN 371S   **Managerial Communications**

This course aims at improving the speaking, writing, listening, and facilitating skills of students who are, or aspire to be, supervisors and managers. *Prerequisite: EN 111 and EN 112. Oral expression competency.* (3 credits, 6 weeks)

ENVIRONMENTAL STUDIES (ES)

ES 111S   An Overview of Environmental Studies
An introduction to the broad field of environmental studies, including worldviews and the nature of scientific inquiry, the relationship between science and religion, earth science, the biological foundations of life, ecology, and resource management and conservation. *Natural science credit.* (3 credits, 5 weeks)

GENERAL EDUCATION (GE)

GE 250S   Foundations for Adult Program Success
This course is designed to prepare the adult student for academic success in the accelerated program format in the School of Adult and Graduate Studies. Includes an introduction to the concepts of groups, critical thinking and problem solving, personal management, worldview, and adult learning as well as the foundational written and oral communications skills needed in the program. (3 credits, 5 weeks)

HISTORY (HS)

HS 111S   Major Issues in World Civilization
A study of the major periods in world history, with primary attention given to western civilization and the western intellectual tradition and their impact on the rest of the world. (3 credits, 5 weeks)

HS 112P   Western Intellectual Tradition: From Leonardo to Hegel
This course is a study of the development of ideas from the Renaissance to the opening of the nineteenth century. Essentially, the course is a history of the life of ideas, and as such necessarily it is an intellectual history covering a period of four centuries, during which the world transformed from medieval to modern. Special focus is given to invention; to inductive scientific method; to political, social, and religious ideas; and to the ideas of a selective few individuals who most contributed to this transformation of society into secularized states. (3 credits, 5 weeks)

HS 211S   Early American History
This course examines European expansion and discovery of the North American continent; the British colonization of the Eastern seaboard; the colonial identity shaped by an amalgamation of African, Native American, and European cultures; and the American Revolution as a manifestation of the liberalism that shaped world history in the modern age. Specific attention is given to how Western race and gender prescriptions shaped the social framework of colonial America and underscored the complex interactions among colonial peoples. (3 credits, 5 weeks)

HS 353S   History of Christianity
A survey of the Christian movement in history, its beliefs, institutions, and worldwide expansion. Attention will be given to doctrinal and ecclesial development, spirituality and devotional practices, historical expressions of service and ministry, and the dynamic between the church and global societies from the ancient world to the present day. *Pre-requisites: HS 111S or permission of professor.* (3 credits, 5 weeks)

HUMAN DEVELOPMENT (HD)

HD 211S   Human Growth and Development
This course is designed to acquaint students with the miraculous passage through the human life span. Through successful completion of this course, students will be better equipped to understand how they and those with whom they interact have progressed and will continue to progress through the life span. Application objectives and outcomes of this course will, ideally, result in the improvement of health, well-being, livelihood, and relationships. *Social science credit.* (3 credits, 5 weeks)

HD 307P   Leadership and Group Dynamics
A study of leadership and group behavior as viewed through experiential group processes, individual interaction, and theory. Content includes the theory and practice of group dynamics and the fundamentals of effective leadership. Particular emphasis will be placed on working towards a general theory of leadership and discovering its applications in a group setting. (3 credits, 5 weeks)

INTERDISCIPLINARY STUDIES (IS)

IS 202S   Christian and Secular Worldviews
A survey of the development and characteristics of common worldviews, including comparing and contrasting the Christian worldview with popular secular worldviews. *Humanities credit.* (3 credits, 5 weeks)

IS 310S   Pre-Internship
The purpose of this course is to prepare students for the practicum/ internship experience. Topics included are internship selection, making the most of the internship, resume building, and facing internship challenges. *Pre-requisite: completion of all major course besides PY 441S & PY 490S.* (3 credits, 5 weeks)

IS 461S   Seminar on Faith and Life
This course is designed to help students define their personal Christian philosophy of life by integrating faith and learning. Students are challenged to explore their Christian calling and to consider ways in which they can exert a Christian influence in the world today. Bachelor degree-seeking only. (3 credits, 5 weeks)

MATHEMATICS (MT)

MT 102S   Mathematics for Management
An examination of various concepts of basic algebra, which assist in building skills for performing specific mathematical operations and problem solving. Specific applications in accounting, finance, and economics are demonstrated and discussed. (3 credits, 6 weeks)

MT 103P   Introduction to Mathematical Concepts
This course is a brief but comprehensive introduction to mathematics. The student will be primarily encouraged to develop mathematical thinking skills, and to understand their uses especially in science and business. This course does contain algebra, trigonometry, calculus, and business math components. After completion, students should have a good conceptual understanding of many fields in mathematics, and be sufficiently skilled to understand how mathematical problems can be approached and solved. (3 credits, 5 weeks)

MT 122S   Elementary Statistics
This course is designed to educate students in the development of statistical thinking. Students will acquire the ability to accurately describe and depict data, make reliable inferences from data, and critically assess the reported results of a variety of statistical studies. Students will use scientific calculators to compute measurements used in a variety of statistical methods and tools. Example application areas include business, psychology, medicine, sports, and the sciences. (3 credits, 6 weeks)

MUSIC (MS)

MS 202P   A Social History of Rock and Roll
This course explores the development of the rock-and-roll phenomenon from its roots in rhythm and blues, jazz and swing and country western music to its maturity and popularity in the latter part of the twentieth century. Carious genres that have been viewed as sub categories or rock-and-roll are defined and examined. A study of influential and popular rock-and-roll musicians, their lives, and their music are included. The course also examines the social and political forces that spawned and nourished this influential genre of music, and also analyzed the effect that rock-and-roll has had on society. Christian principles in relation to participation in rock-and-roll will also be discussed as well as how rock-and-roll has affected the Christian community. *Humanities credit.* (3 credits, 5 weeks)

MS 204P   Red, Hot, and Blue: A Look at American Musical Theater
This course covers the history and development of American musical theater from 1927 through the present and also the creation and production of a musical. Scripts and scores, audio and video recordings, and when possible, live performances and/or rehearsals will supplement text materials. *Humanities credit.* (3 credits, 5 weeks)

MS 205P   Music in the U. S.
From the music of Stephen Foster, and Civil War ballads and bands, to Blues, Bluegrass, Jive and Jazz. Wiley Hitchcock's classic text *Music in the U.S.* guides us as we study, listen, and attend live performances. Then hear guest lectures from folk and jazz artists and country-western songwriters from Nashville, Tennessee. Everything you always wanted to know about music in our country but were afraid to listen to. *Humanities credit.* (3 credits, 5 weeks)

PHILOSOPHY (PH)

PH 301S   Ethics
This course will introduce students to several major ethical theories, including: virtue, rule, and consequential approaches. Students will read and study several important ethical thinkers, both Christian and secular. These ethical theories will then be applied to case studies in a variety of fields such as: bioethics, political ethics, ecclesial ethics, ethics of counseling, business ethics, environmental ethics, etc.
Humanities credit. (3 credits, 5 weeks)

PHYSICAL EDUCATION (PE)

PE 110S   Healthful Living
This course will deal with an overview of the development and maintenance of a healthy lifestyle. Within the context of a historical, scientific, and scriptural basis for human health, students will conduct a fitness assessment and then research and develop a personal plan for physical wellness. Topics will include disease prevention, cardiovascular and strength training, weight management, social support, stress reduction, and personal responsibility. (2 credits, 4 weeks)

PHYSICS (PC)

PC 111S   Matter and Energy
A survey of the development of the concepts of matter and energy within the disciplines of chemistry and physics, with an emphasis on modern applications to the earth and beyond. *Natural science credit.* (3 credits, 5 weeks)

PREACHING (PR)

PR 310S   Biblical Preaching and Communication
This course is designed to give a broad overview of the basic tools and techniques necessary for preparing and presenting sermons based on biblical texts. Topics include an introduction to sermon research as well as what it means to preach in a contemporary context, including the use and misuse of technology ,film, music ,object lessons and a variety of preaching techniques including both narrative and expositional. *Oral expression competency.* (3 credits, 5 weeks)

PR 410S   Preparing for the Gospel Ministry
This course lays the foundation from which effective evangelism will be launched. The class accomplishes this in three stages. The first centers on mastering the very message of the Gospel centered on the cross and resurrection of Jesus and developing skills in sharing the Gospel with others. The second lesson takes seriously the topic of sin: its origins as recounted in the Bible, its consequences in the eternal life of the individual and its systemic effects in the world, and our need of Christ's saving death and resurrection. The third stage focuses on the Great Commission as found in Matthew 28:16-20 as the central evangelical ordinance given to all believers and to become aware of the presence and power of Christ within it. (3 credits, 5 weeks)

PR 420S   Preaching the Gospel
This course teaches how to effectively communicate the gospel message in preaching. With the Bible as the foundation, students will develop understanding in the essential qualities and preparation of an evangelistic message understanding contextual dynamics which affect an effective presentation of the Gospel, the skills necessary to delivering the Gospel in a winsome and effective way, and appropriate and effective methods for inviting people to respond to the Gospel message. *Prerequisite: PR 410S.* (3 credits, 5 weeks)

PR 430S   Prayer and the Holy Spirit
The power of communicating the Gospel message effectively resides in the operations of the Holy Spirit and the prayer life of the presenter. This course explores in-depth the person and work of the Holy Spirit in evangelism as well as the key elements of effectual prayer. Students

will reflect on the movement of the Holy Spirit in their lives as they develop a plan for prayer in their ministries. Some attention will be given to the nature of spiritual warfare and the call to personal holiness. *Prerequisite: PR 420S.* (3 credits, 5 weeks)

PR 491S Seminar on Ministry
Students will meet in a one week intensive format (3 hours per day for five days) to discuss current issues in ministry and church administration. This course will cover topics of church growth, administration, worship, as well as trends and issues in ministry in a seminar style format. *Prerequisite: PR 430S.* (1 credit, 1 week)

PSYCHOLOGY (PY)

PY 201S   Psychology Applied to Modern Life
This course offers majors and non-majors an opportunity to apply knowledge from psychology to practical problems. It provides students with an overview of the theory and research in psychology that is related to the demands and challenges of everyday life. Students examine issues that affect their own adjustment to modern life. The following topics will be addressed: stress, physical health, love relationships, gender, communications, self, personality, work, and development. *Students who earn credit for PY 201 may not earn credit for PY 202. Social science credit.* (3 credits, 5 weeks)

PY 202P   General Psychology
This course is a basic survey of the discipline of psychology: the science of behavior and mental processes. We will examine the physiological, intellectual, emotional, and social aspects of human behavior and look at the applications of psychological theory and research to daily living. *Students who earn credit for PY 202 may not earn credit for PY 201. Social science credit.* (3 credits, 5 weeks)

PY/HU 300S   Child and Adolescent Development
An overview of the physiological, cognitive, psychosocial, and spiritual aspects of development from conception through age 18. *Prerequisite: PY 201S or PY 202P and a minimum of sophomore standing.* (3 credits, 5 weeks)

PY/HU 305S   Adult Development and Aging
An overview of the physical, cognitive, social, spiritual, and emotional aspects of adult development. *Pre-requisites: PY 201S or PY 202P and a minimum of sophomore standing.* (3 credits, 5 weeks)

PY 310S   Research Methods
This course is designed for upper level undergraduate students majoring in human services and psychological studies. The course will provide an introduction to research methodology and a basic framework to critically evaluate social and behavioral science research. You will be exposed to and tested on the major concepts and methods for generating hypotheses and designing a multi-measure study. This course should enable you to evaluate more critically the claims of "experts" in the popular press as well as in the scientific literature. It will also serve as preparation for graduate-level research. *Pre-requisite: PY 201S or PY 202P.* (3 credits, 5 weeks)

PY 314S   Personality
Basic principles of personality structure, dynamics, development, assessment, and theory are discussed. Consideration is given to both the environmental and biological determinants of personality. *Pre-requisite: PY 201S or PY 202P.* (3 credits, 5 weeks)

PY/HU 315S   Abnormal Psychology

A survey of the current categories of abnormal behavior emphasizing symptoms, major theories of causality, and current treatment methods. *Pre-requisite: PY 201S or PY 202P.* (3 credits, 5 weeks)

PY 320S   Social Psychology

The study of the behaviors and thoughts of individuals as influenced by actual or perceived social factors and other individuals. *Pre-requisites: PY 201S or PY 202P.* (3 credits, 5 weeks)

PY/HU 412S   Theories and Principles of Counseling

An examination of several of the major theories of counseling in working with individuals, families, and small groups. Included are principles and techniques utilized in assessment, crisis intervention, contracts, and development of the therapeutic relationship. A skills component is also included. *Pre-requisite: PY 201S or PY 202P.* (3 credits, 5 weeks)

PY/HU 416   Learning and Memory

This course provides a basic overview of the principles, theories and applications of learning and memory. We will cover basic research, theory and applications in human learning, memory, information processing, verbal learning, conditioning and social learning. The knowledge you take away from this course will be useful to you in a wide variety of settings- not only psychology but also in your own personal and professional worlds. *Prerequisite: PY 201S or PY 202P.* (3 credits, 5 weeks)

PY/HU 441S   Internship

Supervised internship provides the student with the opportunity to integrate classroom instruction with practical on-the-job learning in various areas of psychology related fields. *Pre-requisites: IS 310S and all other major courses besides PY 490S.* (3 credits, 10 weeks)

PY/HU 490S   Senior Seminar

Examines the themes of authenticity, self-actualization, and the application of psychological theory in order to explore major Christian worldview questions (what is success in life, how do I become more Christ like, etc.). *Pre-requisite: All other major courses.* (3 credits, 5 weeks)

SOCIOLOGY (SC)

SC 204S   Introduction to Sociology

This course deals with the general nature and principles of sociology. Special attention is given to the ecological, cultural, and psychosocial forces; and to outstanding social groups; to changing personality under the influences that play upon it through group processes. *Social science credit.* (3 credits, 5 weeks)

SC 205S   Marriage and Family

This course is a study of relationships with the opposite sex from first meeting through marriage, having and rearing a family, and divorce and remarriage. Current American norms and Christian principles for marriage and family life are examined. *Social science credit.* (3 credits, 5 weeks)

SC 311S   Social Welfare and Social Services

This course is a survey of the history and philosophy of social welfare and the values and practice of social services as a profession. *Social science credit.* (3 credits, 5 weeks)

SC 414S   Counseling Adolescents and Families

This course examines several of the major theories of counseling families. Working with adolescents within the context of their families will be given special consideration. The skills of counseling adolescents and families will also be emphasized. *Pre-requisite: PY 201S or PY 202P.* (3 credits, 5 weeks)

SPANISH (SP)

SP 101P**Elementary Spanish**

This course is for those who have had less than two years of high school Spanish. Emphasis is upon fundamentals of grammar, vocabulary, composition, pronunciation, and conversation. *Humanities credit.* (3 credits, 6 weeks)

YOUTH AND FAMILY MINISTRIES (YM)

YM 303S**Discipleship and Lifestyle Evangelism**

This course focuses on individual experiences in discipleship, personal sanctification, and evangelism in contemporary society. Special attention will be given to the art of persuasion and its link to communication theory. The importance of perseverance in the faith of those who come to know Christ through evangelistic efforts is ultimately highlighted. (3 credits, 5 weeks)

YM 380S**Administrative Ministry and Organization**

This course will equip students in both the theory and practice of administrative leadership. Many challenges in ministry exist, and one of the most significant is the discipline required to lead and administer well. This course is designed to serve as an overview of practical administrative and leadership issues in ministry in order to prepare students with the tools necessary to organize and oversee various programs across the age ranges. (3 credits, 5 weeks)

YM 401S**Spiritual Formation and Faith Development**

A course to equip students in both the theory and practice of the spiritual disciplines. This course focuses on our personal relationship with God. We will seek to develop an understanding of the necessary aspects of personal spiritual maturation through the evaluation of Scripture and through self-reflection and practice. Second, this course will emphasize theories about the stages of faith and moral development as those theories relate to Christ-centered ministries. (3 credits, 5 weeks)

Course Descriptions for the School of Adult and Graduate Studies: Graduate

Course Numbering System and Abbreviations

Courses numbered 500 are graduate level and are open to students enrolled in a master's program.

BS	Business	**EV**	Environmental Education
CN	Counseling	**GE**	General Education
CS	Computer Studies	**ML**	Management & Leadership

Not every course listed in the Catalog will be offered each year. Students will receive a schedule of classes for their program from their Academic Advisor.

BUSINESS ADMINISTRATION (BS)

BS 530   ETHICS AND THE LEGAL ENVIRONMENT
This is a survey of legal and ethical issues facing management in complex global business situations. Legal and ethical questions are addressed in a case study method, with alternative approaches and solutions analyzed and evaluated. Traditional ethical theories are studied and applied to contemporary business decisions. Students are encouraged to adopt a stakeholder approach that considers the broad ramifications of business actions. This course examines, analyzes, and applies the nature, formation, and system of law in the United States, corporate codes of conduct, and methods of communicating and enforcing ethical expectations. (3 credits, 8 weeks)

BS/CS 536   ANALYSIS OF MIS
This course is designed to thoroughly educate the graduate student in business with the significant role that information systems play as tools used to improve organizational productivity and profitability. Operational, decision-making, and strategic uses of IT are examined.
(4 credits, 8 weeks)

BS 545   CURRENT ECONOMIC ANALYSIS
This course is designed to help students apply economic analysis in practical management decision-making situations. An effort has been made to minimize the use of advanced math and statistics, while still allowing the student to use graphical analysis, statistical concepts, and results of statistical analysis to solve managerial problems. *Prerequisite: BS 351 Economics: Theory, Concepts, and Issues of Micro and Macro or the equivalent.* (3 credits, 8 weeks)

BS 550   FINANCIAL MANAGEMENT PRACTICES
The course is designed to provide students with financial decision-making skills by examining in detail the relationships between financial markets and institutions. Issues related to liquidity, risk management, receivables, payables, cash flow, and capital budgeting are explored. Selected topics in capital valuations, mergers, takeovers, and reorganizations are evaluated. *Prerequisite: BS 422 Issues in Corporate Finance, ML 524 Accounting and Financial Skills for Leadership, or the equivalent.* (3 credits, 8 weeks)

BS 555   ENTREPRENEURSHIP AND SMALL BUSINESS MANAGEMENT
This course is designed to prepare students for the challenges of running a small business or being an entrepreneur. Students are exposed to planning, organizing, and operating a small business or a new venture. Topics include operations, financial planning and e-business. (3 credits, 8 weeks)

BS 560   QUANTITATIVE METHODS IN BUSINESS
This course is designed to provide the graduate student in business with the skills to apply the techniques of quantitative analysis to various types of organizational decision-making situations. *Prerequisite: MT 122S: Statistics* (3 credits, 8 weeks)

BS 565   INTERNATIONAL BUSINESS AND E-COMMERCE
This course is designed to provide information related to global business strategies and e-commerce from a multinational perspective. Included are such topics as exporting, licensing, joint ventures, strategic alliances, counter trading, foreign subsidiaries, and transplant manufacturing facilities as well as the impact of foreign exchange, balance of trade, and international monetary systems. (3 credits, 8 weeks)

BS 570   ADVANCED MANAGERIAL ACCOUNTING

This course examines accounting information from a managerial perspective. Accounting procedures and practices, which include cost/volume/profit analysis, capital expenditure planning, and financial and capital budgeting, as well as project planning and control will be examined. Practical application will be the main focus of study. Use of spreadsheet applications will be encouraged. *Prerequisite: BS 352 Financial Accounting or the equivalent.* (3 credits, 8 weeks)

BS 579   CURRENT ISSUES AND IMPLICATIONS: THE STUDY OF THE EXTERNAL ENVIRONMENT ON INDUSTRY FOR MANAGEMENT PLANNING

This course is designed to explore current issues and recognize trends in the postmodern global business environment. Students will use critical thinking skills and research abilities to predict the global and organizational effects in the field of strategic management. Topics include technology, entrepreneurship, quality, ethics, and an ongoing list of contemporary issues that make up the external environment that organizations operate in. (3 credits, 8 weeks)

BS 580   STRATEGIC PLANNING AND RESEARCH ANALYSIS

This course is designed to integrate the functional areas of business and provide planning skills necessary for improving market share for immediate and future profitability. The strategic planning process is evaluated with emphasis on environmental, social, legal, and market dynamics. Case studies will be utilized, and empirical research will be presented to the class. (3 credits, 8 weeks)

BS 590   MANAGEMENT CONSULTING

An integrative capstone real-world learning experience in management consulting, taken in a joint effort with the regional North Carolina Small Business Technology Development Centers (SBTDC) in Charlotte and Asheville. Students are required to apply knowledge and skills acquired during the program to the business problems of a real-world organization. *Prerequisite: BS 580 and completion of all other MBA course work.* (3 credits, 8 weeks)

CLINICAL MENTAL HEALTH COUNSELING (CN)

CN 600   PROFESSIONAL ORIENTATION TO COUNSELING

This course will be an introductory exploration of the history of counseling as a profession as well as current trends in the practice of clinical mental health counseling. Students will begin to explore the various settings in which counseling can take place and the specialties within the profession, in addition to professional counseling licensure and credentialing. Additional topics covered in this course in an introductory way include counselor self-care, consultation, professional counseling organizations, advocacy, ethics, and multicultural competency. (3 credit, 8 weeks)

CN 605   ETHICS AND ETHICAL PRACTICE IN COUNSELING

This course will examine ethical standards and ethical decision making for the practice of counseling. Applicable codes of ethics will be examined and case studies will be used to challenge students to think critically about ethics and ethical decision making. Ethical issues in individual, group, family, and couples counseling will be covered, as well as multicultural considerations. The course will also address confidentiality, informed consent, boundaries, multiple relationships, supervision, and consultation within an ethical framework. (3 credits, 8 weeks)

CN 610   THEORIES & TECHNIQUES IN COUNSELING

This course will provide an overview of counseling theories and related techniques including psychoanalytic, gestalt, behavioral, cognitive, reality, existential, Adlerian, family systems, feminist, and postmodern therapies. Students will have the opportunity to role play and demonstrate beginning skills for counseling through videotaped role play sessions with classmates. (3 credits, 8 weeks)

CN 615   COUNSELING SKILLS

This course will provide students an opportunity to continue to develop counseling *microskills* as well as foundational skills in interviewing in the helping professions. Students will videotape role-played sessions and participate in peer review as well as review with course instructor. (3 credits, 8 weeks)

CN 620   SPIRITUALITY & RELIGION IN COUNSELING

This course will examine the role of spirituality and religious beliefs in the counseling relationship and process. Students will explore how different religious traditions that clients may participate in could influence the counseling process as well as examine their own religious and spiritual foundations for their counseling theory and practice. Ethical standards will be discussed. (3 credits, 8 weeks)

CN 625   COUNSELING ACROSS THE LIFESPAN

This course will provide an overview of human development across the lifespan, from birth until death and explore critical considerations for counseling individuals across these stages of development. (3 credits, 8 weeks)

CN 630   MULTICULTURAL COUNSELING

This course will provide students an opportunity to begin to develop skills for multicultural competency when providing counseling services to clients of diverse backgrounds. Multicultural competencies will be reviewed and students will explore their own identity as a cultural being. (3 credits, 8 weeks)

CN 635   MENTAL HEALTH DIAGNOSIS AND TREATMENT

This course will provide students an overview of clinical diagnoses according to the current Diagnostic Statistical Manual (DSM V). Diagnosis criteria will be reviewed and current best practice treatment options will be reviewed. Case studies will be utilized to provide students opportunities to practice diagnostic skills. Treatment planning in counseling will also be discussed (3 credits, 8 weeks)

CN 640   CAREER COUNSELING

This course will provide an introductory exploration of career development across the lifespan, career counseling theories, assessments relevant to career counseling, and occupational information sources. The course will allow students opportunity to role play, consider case studies, and create a career intervention for a chosen population. (3 credits, 8 weeks)

CN 645   ASSESSMENT IN COUNSELING

This course will provide an overview of assessment methods and tools used in counseling, including intakes as well as standardized assessments. Ethical standards for the use of assessments in counseling will be reviewed. Students will experience taking an assessment as well as provide a critical review of assessments. (3 credits, 8 weeks)

CN 650   GROUP COUNSELING

This course will provide an overview of theory and principles of effective group work, provide students an opportunity to develop skills in using group techniques, and plan activities for groups. Students will participate in a group experience during this course. Ethical standards for group counseling will be reviewed. (3 credits, 8 weeks)

CN 655   RESEARCH METHODS IN COUNSELING
This course will provide an overview of qualitative and quantitative research methodology and techniques and discuss the role of research in counseling. Ethical standards for conducting research will be discussed. Students will develop the ability to read and critically evaluate counseling literature as well as develop a research prospectus. (3 credits, 8 weeks)

CN 660   CRISIS INTERVENTION/CRISIS COUNSELING
This course will provide students with an overview of counseling skills for working in crisis and trauma situations as well as crisis intervention theory. Students will review case studies and create a crisis resource for a client population or counseling setting of interest. (3 credits, 8 weeks)

CN 665   SUBSTANCE ABUSE COUNSELING
This course will provide an overview of the nature of substance use, abuse, and dependency. Education, prevention, treatment, and recovery will be addressed. (3 credits, 8 weeks)

CN 670   GENDER ISSUES IN COUNSELING
This course will examine the impact of gender on the counseling relationship as well as how gender dynamics can impact the counseling process. (3 credits, 8 weeks)

CN 675   COUNSELING PRACTICUM
This is an experiential course and requires students to complete a minimum of 100 hours of clinical counseling practice, under supervision, at an approved site. Students will provide counseling services as well as continue to learn skills in intake, assessment, counseling, and consultation. Students will participate in weekly individual as well as group supervision. *Pre-requisites: Permission of program director.* (3 credits, 10 weeks)

CN 680   COUNSELING INTERNSHIP I
This is an experiential course and requires students to complete a minimum of 300 hours of clinical counseling practice, under supervision, at an approved site. Students will provide counseling services as well as continue to learn skills in intake, assessment, counseling, and consultation. Students will also begin to complete paperwork required for licensure as an LPC-A (Licensed Professional Counselor Associate) in NC. Students will participate in weekly individual supervision as well as group supervision. *Pre-requisites: CN 675; permission of program director.* (6 credits, 14 weeks)

CN 685   COUNSELING INTERNSHIP II
This is an experiential course and requires students to complete a minimum of 300 hours of clinical counseling practice, under supervision, at an approved site. Students will provide counseling services as well as continue to learn skills in intake, assessment, counseling, and consultation. Students will also begin to complete paperwork required for licensure as an LPC-A (Licensed Professional Counselor Associate) in NC. Students will participate in weekly individual supervision as well as group supervision. *Pre-requisites: CN 680; permission of program director.* (6 credits, 14 weeks)

CN 690   COUNSELING INTERNSHIP III
Repeatable internship credits, if needed.
Pre-requisites: CN 685; permission of program director. (3 credits, 8 weeks)

CN 695 COUNSELING INTERNSHIP IV
Repeatable internship credits, if needed.
Pre-requisites: CN 690; permission of program director. (3 credits, 8 weeks)

ENVIRONMENTAL EDUCATION (EV)

EV 500   FUNDAMENTALS IN ENVIRONMENTAL EDUCATION DESCRIPTION
This web-based course (Internet delivery) provides a foundational knowledge of environmental education and the skills to become an effective environmental educator. This course introduces the learner to theory and practice of EE. Through foundational readings, on-line discussion groups, and projects, students develop a better understanding of environmental education and the skills needed to develop and improve as an environmental educator. (Spring Semester: Year One; 3 credits)

EV 505   INTRODUCTION TO THE MASTER OF SCIENCE IN ENVIRONMENTAL
**   EDUCATION (MSEE)**
Orients students to the nature of graduate study in environmental education at Montreat College. It focuses on cohort building, the educational outcomes of the MSEE, and the mission of the College. Students will also be introduced to related opportunities including N.C. certification in environmental education, off campus field courses, and elective options. After discussing the program philosophy, course sequence, program delivery model (online work and summer/weekend intensives), issues related to graduate study, and other opportunities, students will develop a comprehensive plan for completion of the MSEE that incorporates required courses, electives, and other opportunities. (Spring Semester: Year One; 1 credit)

EV 506   RESEARCH PRACTICUM
This practicum will concentrate on the literature review process, as preparation for EV 520 (Research Methods), as well the student's final thesis or project. The class will meet during the summer intensive where key components of a well-written literature review will be defined. After the summer intensive, a student will work independently with a professor on preparing a literature review, so that the student is ready to think about research methods related to a specific question. (First Summer; 1 credit)

EV 510   INSTRUCTIONAL STRATEGIES IN ENVIRONMENTAL EDUCATION
Emphasizes a wide array of instructional strategies and teaching methods that focus on an inductive approach to learning. Students will develop and practice strategies for making effective instructional decisions, assessing needs, selecting appropriate instructional objectives and evaluating student learning. A variety of specific methods and philosophies relative to environmental education for all ages will be introduced. Successful completion of this course will satisfy the teaching methods workshop requirement for the North Carolina environmental education certification. (Summer Intensive: Year One; 3 credits)

EV 515   EARTH SYSTEMS
This course reviews the structure and function of a variety of environmental systems operating in the atmosphere, hydrosphere, geosphere, cryosphere and biosphere. Physical, chemical, and biological processes will be considered with respect to local, regional, and global levels of scale. Course topics include energy flow, biogeochemical cycles, biomes and biogeographic regions, ecological and physical zonation, the ocean-atmosphere interface, and the notion of change in earth's spheres and zones. (Summer Intensive: Year One; 3 credits)

EV 516   SCIENCE SEMINAR
This course will add to students' environmental content knowledge. Students will learn science content that is seasonally appropriate; topics will include such things as fall overturn in lakes, animal and plant adaptations to winter, and other seasonal changes. The goal is that students will be able to interpret the natural world through the seasons. Students will keep a nature journal throughout the time that the course is taught. (Fall Semester: Year One; 1 credit)

EV 520   RESEARCH METHODS
This course reviews qualitative, quantitative, and mixed methods approaches to research in environmental education. Topics include research design, methods for data collection and analysis, and strategies for completing the final document. Note: This course is not intended to be a statistics course. Those students interested in a quantitative research design for their thesis or final project should take a graduate level statistics course as an elective. (Fall Semester: Year One; 4 credits)

EV 525   DESIGNING ENVIRONMENTAL EDUCATION EXPERIENCES
This course will address concepts using diverse settings for environmental education and how to develop curriculum that meets the needs of the student, agency, state and/or school. Students will design and participate in a variety of integrated environmental education learning experiences including expeditionary science, ecotourism, and field-based immersion experiences. (Fall Semester: Year One; 2 credits)

EV 530   ENVIRONMENTAL HISTORY AND PHILOSOPHY
This course investigates the major philosophical, ethical, and theological strands of thought that have influenced environmental thinking. The course will use the history of the environmental movement as a framework for understanding the development of environmental attitudes, perceptions, and behaviors. Students will develop and revise their own philosophy of environmental education through interaction with the readings and discussion. (Spring Semester: Year Two; 3 credits)

EV 535   ENVIRONMENTAL COMMUNICATIONS
Introduces communication theories as they intersect with environmental education and issues and uses critical methods to analyze these issues. The course will increase awareness of the strategies and arguments used by groups, institutions, the media, and key individuals in communicating environmental information and issues. It will also examine theories of communication in terms of public participation in environmental decision-making. Finally, the course will look at strategies that environmental interpreters have used in translating environmental information into communication formats that make it easier and more compelling for the public to understand the information. (Spring Semester: Year Two; 3 credits)

EV 540   SURVEY OF ENVIRONMENTAL EDUCATION RESOURCES
Students will investigate instructional resources for K-12 environmental education and then evaluate and apply them to their practice. Course will include the resources needed to complete the workshop requirement for the NC certification in environmental education. A culminating project will link resources encountered to grade level taught and individual areas of interest. *This course can be waived if the student can show evidence of a course similar to this taken prior to enrolling in the masters and/or if 7 national environmental education curriculum workshops have been completed during the last 5 years. Waived if student completed OE 220 at Montreat College.* (Spring Semester: Year One; 2 credits)

EV 545   ENVIRONMENTAL ISSUES INVESTIGATION AND ACTION
This course will provide knowledge, skills and opportunity to investigate and evaluate environmental issues. Students will take a leadership role in an environmental action project. Successful completion of this course will satisfy the action project requirement for the North Carolina environmental education certification. **This course can be waived if the student has completed an action project for the NCEE certification program. Student should show proof of completion.** (Summer Semester: Year Two; 1 credit)

EV 550 THESIS PROPOSAL OR PROJECT DESIGN
This course provides students with an opportunity to make an original contribution to the field of environmental education through a thesis or a chance for the student to develop an expert's knowledge of a particular industry segment and to build a network of professional contacts within a specific sub-field through a project. Topics may be explored via two avenues: research thesis or project. Either of these forms is acceptable and will be comparable in the amount of work required. (Spring Semester: Year Two; 1 credit)

EV 555 ECOSYSTEMS
Students will have the opportunity to travel and visit field study sites and public education facilities in selected biomes and life zones. Ecosystem comparisons will be developed with attention given to flora and fauna. Special emphasis will be placed on environmental education programs that educate the public on biomes and life zones. Students will travel as a group for this two-week experience. (Summer Semester: Year Two; 3 credits)

EV 560 THESIS/PROJECT PREPARATION
Students will make satisfactory progress toward developing a proposal for the thesis/non-thesis project. The thesis/non-thesis project will be of substantial depth that explores a specific area of environmental education and integrates the MSEE curriculum. This course is subject to repeated registration. Students must receive a satisfactory grade (S) before a student enrolls in EV 570. (Summer Semester: Year Two; 3 credits.)

EV 570 NONRESIDENT THESIS/PROJECT
This course is for non-resident graduate students who have completed all course requirements for the Masters of Science in Environmental Education, but have not completed the thesis/project. Pre-requisite: Satisfactory completion of EV 560. (0 credit) Fee: $500

EV 581 DIRECTED STUDY (1-6)
Directed Study for graduate students enrolled in the Master of Science in Environmental Education. Students may choose to participate in a directed study of their own choice and direction of a faculty member. Credit varies from 1 – 3, although a student can repeat for up to six hours of credit. (Any semester; 1 – 6 credits)

FIRST YEAR GRADUATE EXPERIENCE FOR MBA/MSML (GE)

GE 510 INTRODUCTION TO GRADUATE STUDIES
This course introduces students to graduate studies and the College's Christ-centered mission. Topics covered include the relationship between faith and learning, ethics, stewardship, self-management skills, and collaborative learning. (3 credits, 8 weeks)

MANAGEMENT AND LEADERSHIP (ML)

ML 504 EXPLORING LEADERSHIP AND PERSONAL LEADERSHIP DEVELOPMENT
This course explores leadership traits, styles, roles, and responsibilities of successful leaders over time from Jesus to Jack Welch. This course seeks to determine the students' individual strengths and develop their weaknesses. This course will challenge the students with case study analysis and real world application. (3 credits, 8 weeks)

ML 505 MANAGEMENT CONSULTING SERVICE PROJECT
This course provides an introduction to the theory and practice of management consultancy and considers both the consulting process and industry. The course is aimed at management students who undertake a management service project as a capstone learning activity for their degree program. Each student will prepare a proposal for a service project to develop

147

and apply management and leadership skills in a real-world scenario. Demonstrated skills include project management, analysis, and relationship-building. (3 credits, 8 weeks)

ML 510   ORGANIZATIONAL BEHAVIOR

Drawn from the behavioral and social sciences, this course examines leadership theories and management issues. Students examine leadership behaviors, business relationships, personnel assessment, cultural diversity, organizational stresses, team and group dynamics and other organizational issues influencing management decisions. (3 credits, 8 weeks)

ML 512   HUMAN CAPITAL MANAGEMENT

This course explores the critical issues in human resources strategy, leading the organization's most important assets and developing and keeping people. Students will research diversity training programs, best methods for identifying and developing leaders, optimizing organizational performance and compensation programs for effectiveness. (3 credits, 8 weeks)

ML 515   EFFECTIVE COMMUNICATION, NEGOTIATING AND CONFLICT RESOLUTION

This course surveys the latest theories, models, research, and best practices related to effective communication, conflict resolution, and negotiation. Communication within organizations, between individuals, and to the public is explored through discussing interpersonal skills and the telecommunication mediums that are used formally and informally. (3 credits, 8 weeks)

ML 524   ACCOUNTING AND FINANCIAL SKILLS FOR LEADERSHIP

This course seeks to provide students with an understanding of the basic skills in Accounting and Finance necessary to the business leader. Topics include financial statements, financial statement analysis, budgeting, and time value of money. (4 credits, 8 weeks)

ML 540   MARKETING STRATEGIES FOR MANAGERS AND LEADERS

This course is an integrated approach to planning and implementing marketing strategies and tactics from a management perspective with an emphasis on the discipline of maintaining customer focus in highly diverse local and global markets. The course covers the review of marketing principles by which products and services are designed to meet customer needs and priced, promoted, and distributed to the end users. The course also examines the theory and application of Internet marketing. (3 credits, 8 weeks)

ML 542   STRATEGIC PLANNING

This course is designed to integrate the functional areas of an organization, examine the external and internal environments in which they operate and provide planning skills necessary for setting a competitive strategy. The strategic plan is studied as a proactive and reactive process and students have the opportunity to conduct empirical research and develop a plan for business, non-profits or community involvement activities/events. (4 credits, 8 weeks)

ML 585   ADVANCED ENTREPRENEURSHIP AND THE INTRAPRENEURIAL SPIRIT

This is a capstone course designed to integrate all courses. Students will develop a business plan for a real entrepreneurial venture or design an *intrapreneurial* solution to a current leadership issue or community plan. This course prepares the student for the challenges of running a small business or being a leader in an organization or major project. Students are exposed to planning, organizing, and operating a business and incorporating the skills developed as an individual, working with others, the open organizational system and developing a competitive advantage in this final project. *Pre-requisites: All other courses in MSML program.* (4 credits, 8 weeks)

2016-2017 Administrative Officers and Cabinet

Paul J. Maurer (2014) ....President
      B.A., University of Cincinnati
      M.Div., Gordon-Conwell Theological Seminary
      Ph.D., Claremont Graduate University
Daniel T. Bennett (2014)...............Vice President for Student Services and Dean of Students
      B.A., Biola University
      M.A., Wheaton College
      Ph.D., Clemson University
Susan DeWoody (2015) ....Vice President and Dean for Adult and Graduate Studies
      B.S., Arkansas Tech University
      M.S., Northeastern State University
      Ed.D. (In progress), Dallas Baptist University
Jack H. Heinen (2014) ....Vice President for Finance and Administration
      B.A., Dordt College
      M.B.A., Harvard Business School
Kristin Janes (2015) ....Vice President for Enrollment Management
      B.A., North Park University
      M.O.L., University of Northwestern
Gregory P. Kerr (2015) ....Vice President for Academic Affairs & Dean of the College
      B.S., Cornell University
      M.S., Colorado State University
      Ph.D., University of Minnesota
Joseph B. Kirkland (2007) ....Counselor to the President
      B.S., University of Southern Mississippi
      M.A., Lancaster Bible College
Alex Miller (2015) ....Vice President for Advancement
      D.A., Mars Hill University
      M.A., Southern Baptist Theological Seminary

Faculty Emeriti

Lloyd Davis..Professor Emeritus of Mathematics and Physics
      B.A., M.A., Miami University, Ohio
Charles A. Lance...Administrator Emeritus
      A.S., Montreat College
      B.S., Florida State University
      M.A.Ed., East Carolina State University
John T. Newton..Professor Emeritus of Bible and Philosophy
      B.E.E., Georgia Institute of Technology
      M.Div., Th.M., Columbia Theological Seminary
      Ph.D., Emory University
David L. Parks...Professor Emeritus of Bible
      B.E.E., Georgia Institute of Technology
      M.Div., D.D., Columbia Theological Seminary
James D. Southerland..Professor Emeritus of Art
      B.F.A., East Carolina University
      M.F.A., Pennsylvania State University

Charles Larry Wilson..Academic Dean Emeritus
        B.S., Springfield College
        M.S., State University of New York at Cortland
        Ph.D., Florida State University

2016-2017 Full Time Faculty

Angle, Kimberly G. (2007).............Associate Professor of English, Writing Program Director
        B.A., Mercer University
        M.A., Georgia State University
        Ph.D., University of South Carolina
Armstrong, Noreal (2016)................................Assistant Professor of Counselor Education
        B.S., Stephen F. Austin State University
        M.S., Texas A&M
        Ph.D., University of Texas – San Antonio
Auman, Kevin C. (2008) ....Associate Professor of Music
        B.A., Montreat College
        M.A., University of North Carolina at Greensboro
Blanton, P. Gregory (1997) ....Professor of Human Services
        B.S., Evangel College
        M.Ed., Converse College
        M.Ed., Clemson University
        Ed.D. East Texas State University
Brandenburg, Benjamin B. (2014) ....Assistant Professor of History
        B.A., Northwestern College
        Ph.D. candidate, Temple University
Burgin, Kelli ....Assistant Professor of Cybersecurity
        B.A., University of Northern Iowa
        M.S. Bellevue University
Daniel, R. Bradley (1984) ....Professor of Biology/ES/OE
        B.A., M.A., Appalachian State University
        M.S., Northern Illinois University
        Ph.D., Antioch University
Dukas, Stephen P. (2009) ....Associate Professor of Accounting/Finance
        B.S., Florida State University
        Ph. D., Florida State University
Faircloth, W. Bradley (2011) ....Associate Professor of Psychology
        B.A., M.A., Ph.D., University of Notre Dame
Forstchen, William R. (1993) ....Professor of History, Faculty Fellow
        B.A., Rider College
        M.A., Ph.D., Purdue University
Gray, Richardson K. (1975) ....Professor of English
        B.A., Malone College
        M.A., Ph.D., Ohio University
Hamblin, Penny (2016)...............................Assistant Professor of Counselor Education
        B.A., East Carolina University
        M.A., Argosy University
        Ed.D., Argosy University

Howell, Cynthia M. (2005) ....Associate Professor of English
        B.A., Baylor University
        M.A., Vanderbilt University
        Ph.D., University of Kentucky
Joyce, Brian J. (1996) ....Professor of Biology/ES
        B.S., M.S., Ph.D., Pennsylvania State University
Kalisch, Kenneth R. (2008) ....Associate Professor of Outdoor Education
        B.S., University of Nebraska at Omaha
        M.S., Minnesota State University
Kamer, M. Shane (2014) ....Assistant Professor of Exercise Science
        B.S., Shawnee State University
        B.S., D.C., Logan University
King, Don W. (1974) ....Professor of English
        B.A., Virginia Polytechnic Institute
        M.A., Southern Illinois University
        Ph.D., University of North Carolina at Greensboro
King, Nathan (2013) ....Information Technology Services Librarian
        B.A., Montreat College
        M.L.S., North Carolina Central University
Konarski-Fusetti, Monica (2001) ....Instructor of English
        B.A., M.A., East Carolina University
Lassiter, Mark T. (1992) ....Professor of Biology/ES
        B.S., M.A., College of William and Mary
        Ph.D., North Carolina State University
Mullert, Mark B. (2014) ....Assistant Professor of Outdoor Education
        B.S., Houghton College
        M.S., State University of New York at Cortland
Nelson, Lotes (2015)..Assistant Professor of Counselor Education
        B.S., Montreat College
        M.S., Ph.D., Walden University
Neuzil, Linda (2015)............................... Director of Teacher Education/Associate Professor
        B.A., Judson University
        M.Ed., National-Louis University
        Ed.D., Northern Illinois University
Owen, Paul L. (2001) ....Professor of Biblical and Religious Studies
        B.A., Life Pacific College
        M.A., Talbot School of Theology, Biola University
        Ph.D., University of Edinburgh
Owolabi, Isaac B. (1994) ....Professor of Business
        B.S., M.S., University of Wisconsin
        Ph.D., University of Minnesota
Oxenreider, Tom (2008) ....Instructor of Interdisciplinary Studies
        B.A., University of Pittsburgh at Johnstown
        M.B.A., Wheeling Jesuit College
Pearson, Elizabeth R. (1978) .... Professor/Director of the Library
        B.S., University of North Carolina at Greensboro
        M.S.L.S., University of North Carolina at Chapel Hill

Pope, John N. (2016)..........Assistant Professor of Counselor Education, Director of Clinical Mental Health Counseling
    B.A., Stetson University
    M.Div., Columbia Theological Seminary
    Ph.D., Texas A&M University – Corpus Christi
Powell, John N. (2005) ....Associate Professor of Business
Shepson, Donald R. (2005) ....Associate Professor of Bible and Religion
    B.A., Wheaton College
    M.Div., Gordon Conwell Theological Seminary
    Ph.D., Talbot School of Theology, Biola University
Shuman, Dorothea K. (1996)......................................Professor of OE/Environmental Studies
    B.S.Ed., State University College at Cortland
    M.S., Pennsylvania State University
    Ph.D., University of Idaho
Smith, Benjamin S. (2014) ....Assistant Professor of Music Business
    B.A., B.S., Florida State University
    M.M., University of Miami
    J.D., University of Memphis
Taylor, David L. (2013) ....Dean of Spiritual Formation
    B.A., King College
    M.Div., Columbia Theological Seminary/University of Glasgow, Scotland
    M.Th., Princeton Theological Seminary
    D.Min., Talbot School of Theology
Teo, Jeff Y. (2004) ....Professor of Cybersecurity
    B.S., M.S., Western New England College
    Ed.S., Ph.D., Nova Southeastern University
    CISSP, CEH, Security+, Network+ and A+
Toland, Lisa (2016).................... Associate Professor of History, Director of Honors Program
    B.A., Indiana Wesleyan University
    M.A., Miami University of Ohio
    M.St., D.Phil., University of Oxford, Jesus College
Webb, George R. Jr. (2015) ....Instructor of Mathematics
    B.A., University of North Carolina, Asheville
    M.A., Western Carolina University
Wells, Mark A. (2006) ....Professor of Ethics/Philosophy
    B.A., Friends University
    M.A., Fuller Theological Seminary
    Ph.D., Baylor University
White-Hinman, Callan (2007) ....Professor of Theatre Arts
    B.A., DeSales University
    M.F.A., California State University, Long Beach
Wilds, Timothy (2009) ....Assistant Professor of Music
    B.M., Covent College
    M.M., Westminster Choir College
Wilson, Melissa (2015)................................Instructor of Environmental & Natural Science
    B.A., M.S., Montreat College

2016-2017 Part-Time Pro Rata Faculty

Hernandez, Horacio A. (2004)...Associate Professor of Spanish
        B.A., Universito Autonoma de Santo Domingo
        M.A., Ph.D., University of New York at Albany

Southerland, James D. (1987) ....Artist in Residence, Professor Emeritus of Art, Faculty Fellow
        B.F.A., East Carolina University
        M.F.A., Pennsylvania State University

Stackhouse, Eunice W. (1996) ....Professor of Music
        B.M.E., Grace College
        M.M., Indiana University School of Music
        D.M.A., University of Kansas

2016-2017 Adjunct Faculty

School of Adult and Graduate Studies

Adams, Nolan (Scott)   Business, Computer
B.A., Montreat College
M.B.A., Baker College
Ph.D., Capella University

Ave'Lallemant, Timothy   Mathematics
B.A., University of Wisconsin
M.S., Institute of Paper Chemistry
M.S., University of Akron

Avery, Courtnay   Business
B.A., North Carolina Wesleyan
MBA, DeVry University
M.S., DeVry University

Bailey, Connie   Business
B.S., Pfeiffer University
M.S., Pfeiffer University

Bannister, John   Business
B.S., Strayer University
M.B.A., University of Phoenix

Barron, Sue   English
B.A., Mars Hill College
M.A., Western Carolina University

Bayode, Bola   Business
B.S., Ogun State University
M.B.A., Strayer University
Ph.D., Walden University

Blue, Lucinda   Business
B.A., Johnson C. Smith University
MBA, Winthrop University
Ph.D., The Union Institute

Boer, Robert   Music
B.C.S., Redeemer College
M.M., Drake University
D.M.A., University of Iowa

Boyce, Jeff   Business
B.S., Michigan Technological University
M.B.A., Ashland University
Ph.D., Capella University

Brandon, Paul   Business
B.S., California Institute of Technology
M.A., Harvard University
Ph.D., Harvard University

Busby, Walter (Buzz)   Business Law
B.S., Louisiana State University
J.D. Law, Louisiana State University

Canfora, Jennifer   Counseling
B.S., UNC-Greensboro
M.A., Webster University
Ph.D., Capella University

Carlin, Eve   Business Law
B.A., St. Clairs College
M.A., Marist College
J.D. Law, Hofstra University

Cellamare, Alan   Business
B.A., University of South Florida
M.B.A., Seattle University
M.Div., Gordon Conwell
D.Min., Gordon Conwell

Chabra, Nicolas   Business
B.A., Farleigh Dickinson University
J.D., George Mason University

Chuprevich, Robert   Bible, Business
B.S., Bryant College
M.S., Western Carolina University
D.Min., Erskine Theological Seminary

Clark, Matthew   Mathematics
B.A., Clemson University
M.S., Columbia University
Ph.D., North Carolina State University

Corbitt, Chris   Science
B.A., North Carolina State University
M.S., East Carolina University

Corbitt, Lisa   Science
B.S., North Carolina State University
M.S., East Carolina University

Davis, Gary   Business
B.S., University of North Carolina
M.A., Western Carolina University
M.S., Western Carolina University
Ph.D., North Carolina State University

Dollar, Julie   Counseling
B.S., Lenoir Rhyne University
M.A., Lenoir Rhyne University

Edwards, Miriam   Spanish
   B.A., Clemson University
   M.A., Winthrop University
Farr, Larry   Music
   B.A., Illinois Wesleyan University
   M.Ed., University of Illinois
Felts, Bennie   Business
   B.A., North Carolina Central
      University
   M.A., Elon College
   Ph.D., Capella University
Fitzpatrick, Troy   Business
   B.S., Troy University
   M.S., Montreat College
Ford, Allison   Counseling
   B.A., Mary Washington College
   M.E., University of Virginia
   Ph.D., University of Virginia
Fox, Joseph   Business
   B.S., Pfeiffer University
   M.B.A., Western Carolina University
   Ed.D., Western Carolina University
Frazier, Bradford   Business
   B.A., Pfeiffer University
   M.B.A., Pfeiffer University
   Ph.D., Lynn University
Gentry, Elizabeth   Accounting
   B.S., Montreat College
   M.A. Gardner Webb University
Gibbs, Mark   Bible and Religion
   B.A., Montreat College
   M.A., Gordon –Conwell University
   Ph.D., University of Wales
Gordon, Michelle   Counseling
   B.S., Appalachian State University
   M.A., Appalachian State University
   Ph.D., Regent University
Gorman, Clint   Business
   B.B.A., Montreat College
   M.B.A., Montreat College
Gorman, Kevin   Business
   B.S., University of Massachusetts
   M.B.A., California State University
   Ph.D., Texas A & M University
Graham, David   Counseling
   B.A., Le Moyne College
   M.S., Syracuse University
   Ph.D., University of North Carolina,
      Charlotte

Gray, Wilma   Social Work
   B.A., Malone College
   M.S.W., University of North Carolina,
      Chapel Hill
   M.A., Western Carolina University
Greenlee, Laura   Psychology
   M.S., Walden University
   M.S., McDaniel College
   Ph.D., Walden University
Griffin, Robert   Business
   B.B.A., Montreat College
   M.B.A., Montreat College
Hall, Robert   History
   B.A., Greenville College
   M.Ed., Florida-Atlantic University
   M.A., University of North Carolina
Harris, Franklin   Communications
   B.A., Eastern Kentucky University
   M.A., Montclair State University
   Ed.D., Rutgers University
Harshaw, Kimberly   Psychology
   B.S., University of North Carolina,
      Greensboro
   M.S., Walden University
Hendrickson, Patricia   Business
   B.B.A., Montreat College
   M.Ed., Francis Marion University
   Ed.D., Fielding Graduate School
Hogsed, Daryle   History
   B.A., Gardner-Webb University
   M.A., Western Carolina University
Hopkins, T. Hampton   Business
   B.S., Winthrop University
   M.S., University of Tennessee,
      Knoxville
   Ed.D., University of North Carolina,
      Charlotte
Howard, Jack   Business, Math,
Science
   B.S., Kings College
   M.A., Queens College
Huddleston-Edwards, Sandra   English
   B.A., University of North Carolina,
      Charlotte
   M.A., University of North Carolina,
      Charlotte
Ingrassia, David   Bible and Religion
   B.A., Tufts University
   Th.M., Dallas Theological Seminary
   D.Min., Dallas Theological Seminary

Irwin, Kathleen   Business
  B.S., University of North Carolina,
     Wilmington
  MBA, University of North Carolina,
     Charlotte
  Ph.D., Capella University
Jordan, Randall   Bible and Religion
  B.S., University of South Carolina
  M.Div., Southern Baptist Theological
     Seminary
  D.Min., Southern Baptist Theological
     Seminary
Kamer, Shane   Science
  B.S., Logan University
  M.S., Logan University
  D.C., Logan College of Chiropractic
Kehres, Patrick   Business
  B.S., University of Phoenix
  M.B.A., University of Phoenix
  D.M., University of Phoenix
Loelius, William   Business
  B.B.A., Montreat College
  M.B.A., Montreat College
Lutz, Janet (2013)   Counseling
  B.A., Hood College
  M.S., Wake Forest University
  Ph.D., University of Florida
Mashburn, Michael   Math
  B.A., UNC Asheville
  M.A., Western Carolina University
Mazzatenta, Ernie   Communication
  B.A., Kent State University
  M.S., Northwestern University
McLaughlin, Shirley   Business
  B.A., University of North Carolina,
     Greensboro
  M.S., Rollins College
  Ph.D., Nova Southeastern University
McMiller, Beniah   Business
  B.S., Johnson C. Smith University
  M.S., Colorado Technical University
  M.S., University of Phoenix
McMiller, Tai   Psychology
  B.A., University of South Carolina
  M.A., Webster University
Mead, Danielle   Counseling
  B.S., Georgia State University
  M.A., Webster University

Morgan, Adam   English
  B.A., Furman University
  M.A., Roosevelt University
Mosely, Jackie   Business
  B.S., Winthrop University
  M.B.A., Winthrop University
Murray, Peter   Business
  B.A., University of Notre Dame
  M.B.A., University of Pennsylvania,
     Wharton School
Mullins, Melissa   Counseling
  B.A., Allen University
  M.A., Webster University
  Ph.D., Argosy University
Njoku, Matthew   Business
  B.S., State University of New York,
     Binghamton
  M.B.A., State University of New York,
     Binghamton
Paul, Eileen   Business
  B.A., College of Mt. Saint Vincent
  M.B.A., University of Wisconsin,
     Milwaukee
Peters, Cindy   Psychology
  B.A., Miami University
  M.A., Kent State University
  Ph.D., Southern Illinois University
Peters, Debra   Psychology
  B.S., East Tennessee State University
  M.A., East Tennessee State
     University
  Ph.D., University of Southern
     Mississippi
Pouler, Chris   Science
  B.S., University of Maryland
  M.A., Catholic University
  Ph.D., University of Maryland
Priddy, Carroll Sue   Business
  B.A., Mars Hill College
  M.S., Western Carolina University
Rajagopal, Sanjay   Business
  B.A., University of Delhi
  MBA, Western Carolina University
  M.A., Jawaharlal Nehru University
  Ph.D., Mississippi State University
Sams, Jeanette   Business
  B.A., Montreat College
  M.A., Western Carolina University

Sanders, Laurie   Business
  B.A., California State University
  M.B.A., City University of London
Sheets, Don   Psychology & Science
  B.S., North Carolina State University
  M.S., Central Michigan University
  Ph.D., LaSalle University
Sherrill, Debra   Business
  B.S., University of North Carolina
  M.B.A., Wingate University
  Ph.D., Capella University
Simmons, I-Eesha   Human Resources
  B.A., UNC-Charlotte
  M.S., Pfeiffer University
  J.D., Massachusetts School of Law
Soirez, Rhonda   Counseling
  B.S., Liberty University
  M.A., Liberty University
Spicuzza, Robert   Science, Math
  B.S., Worcester Polytechnic Institute
  M.S., University of Connecticut
  Ph.D., University of Connecticut
Streppa, Michael   Psychology
  B.A., Dickinson College
  M.A., Georgia School of Professional
      Psychology
  Ph.D., Georgia School of Professional
      Psychology
Summers, LaTonya   Counseling
  B.S., Appalachian State University
  M.A., Appalachian State University
Szelwach, Celia   Business
  B.S., United States Military Academy
  M.B.A., Argosy University
  Ph.D., Argosy University
Taylor, Diana   Psychology
  B.A., University of North Carolina,
      Greensboro
  M.S., Winthrop University
  Ph.D., Regent University
Tonini, Edward   Bible and Religion
  B.A., University of Western Ontario
  M.Div., University of Western
      Ontario
Vining, Chip   Psychology
  B.S., University of Florida
  M.A., Reformed Theological
      Seminary

Wallace, Tom   Business
  B.S., Gardner-Webb University
  M.B.A., Montreat College
Walton, Steven   Music
  B.A., University of Houston
  M.M., The Julliard School
Webb, Kirk   Counseling
  B.A., Wake Forest University
  M.A., Colorado Christian University
  M.A., Princeton Theological
      Seminary
  Ph.D., Seattle Pacific University
Wencel, Mark   Business
  B.S., University of Pittsburgh
  M.A., University of Pittsburgh
Whetstone, Kimarie
      Computer Science
  B.S., University of North Carolina,
      Charlotte
  M.Ed., University of North Carolina,
      Charlotte
Whisnant, Jason   Counseling
  B.S., Gardner Webb University
  Ed.S., Gardner Webb University

Administrative and Professional Staff

School of Arts and Sciences

Chris Anderson	Athletic Trainer
Meghan Austin	Head Women's Basketball Coach
Brenton Benware	Head Men's Soccer Coach
Elena Binder	Financial Aid Counselor
Keri Boer	Director of Records & Registration
Michael Bruce	Assistant Men's Soccer Coach
Kristine Buckwalter	Director of Advancement Services
Adam Caress	Assistant Director of Communications
Annie Carlson	Executive Director of Advancement
Martha Chastain	Assistant Director of Auxiliary Services
Jessica Clements	Assistant to the VP for Academic Affairs & Dean of the College
Andrew Cobb	Director of Tennis
Sara Cole	Director of Student Accounts
Hope Deifell	Executive Assistant to the President
Debbie Ferguson	Director of Development
Katharyn Ferguson	Assistant Women's Lacrosse Coach
Adora Fitzpatrick	Help Desk Administrator
Grace Green	Special Events Coordinator
Patti Guffey	Controller
Paul Hawkinson	Director of Technology
Raymond Henderson	Assistant Men's Basketball Coach
Bethany Holder	Admissions Event Coordinator
Eric Hollandsworth	Creative Director
Jeremy Hurse	Associate Director of Financial Aid
Tyler Johnson	Assistant Women's Basketball
Garrett Jones	Head Men's Basketball Coach
Tom Jones	Admissions Counselor
Kristina Kamer	Head Volleyball Coach
Mickie Kelly	Payroll and Benefits Manager
Nathan King	Information Technology Service Librarian
Jessica Langston	Sr. Asst. Dir. of Records & Registration for SAS and Advising
José Larios	Athletic Director
Tim Lewis	Assistant Men's Basketball Coach
Jason Lewkowicz	Director of Track & Field/Cross Country
Heather Maston	Head Softball Coach
MacKenzie May	Financial Aid Counselor
Andrew McAllister	Assistant Volleyball Coach
Heidi McInturf	Admissions Data Coordinator
Will McMinn	Director of Lacrosse, Head Men's Lacrosse Coach
Grace Miller	Campus Nurse
Daniel Mount	Web Communications Specialist
Courtney Nash	Head Women's Soccer Coach
Sandra Owen	Administrative Assistant to the VP of Student Services
Mandi Pike	Associate Director of Admissions
Beth Pocock	Director of Financial Aid
Teresa Price	Director of Auxiliary Services

Jo Reynolds	Accounting & Administrative Assistant
Kirsten Richardson	Admissions Counselor
John Rogers	Director of the Team and Leadership Center
Gloria Sainio	Enrollment Management Office Assistant
Rebecca Shaw	Library Services Manager
Christian Smith	Admissions Counselor
Denise Smith	Special Assistant to the President
Ryan Smith	Assistant Baseball Coach
John Sullivan	Golf Coach
David Taylor	Chaplain
Lyndsey Wall	Assistant Dean for Residence Life & Anderson RD
Robert Walker	Director of Retail & Auxiliary Revenue
Dave Walters	Director of Alumni, Parent, and Church Relations
Ryan Watkins	Director of Service and Davis RD
Audrey Weaver	Accounts Payable Specialist
Joshua Wilcox	Systems Administrator
Jane Woods	Assistant to the VP of Advancement
Holleigh Woodward	Director of Counseling Services
Joshua Yeatman	Information Systems Support Specialist

School of Adult and Graduate Studies

Elena Binder   Financial Aid Counselor
Keri Boer   Director of Records & Registration
Michael Davis   Director of Admission
Susan DeWoody   Vice President and Dean of Adult and Graduate Studies
Elizabeth Hofheins Records Specialist
Cindy Kirkland   Director of Academic Advising and Student Services
Dr. Eboni Mathis   Director of Online Education
Margót Payne   Associate Director of Records & Registration
Julia Pacilli   Director of Campus and Faculty Services
Jim Paden   Director of AGS Marketing
Beth Pocock   Director of Financial Aid

Asheville Campus

Jesse Boeckermann Admissions Representative
John Carvajal   Academic Advisor for Online
Jennifer Gardner   Administrative Coordinator for AGS
Marcella Gibson   Campus Services Coordinator
Jonathan McDonald Academic Advisor
Dr. Isaac Owolabi   Full time Faculty/Business and Marketing
Lyndsey Parham   Admissions Representative

Charlotte Campus

Latwoia Abbott   Academic Advisor
Mary Banks   Admissions Specialist
Nicole Chavis   Campus Services Coordinator
Monica Konarski-Fusetti Full time Faculty/English
Lotes Nelson   Fulltime Faculty/CMHC
John-Nelson Pope   CMHC Program Director
Laura Ormond   Special Assistant to the President - Charlotte
Rafael Velasquez   Admissions Representative - Charlotte

Extended Campuses

Dr. Penny Hamblin Full time Faculty/Counseling - Morganton
Ethel Kelly   Campus Advisor – NCWC
Jennifer Strickland Academic Advisor – Morganton

Index

www.ingramcontent.com/pod-product-compliance
Lightning Source LLC
Chambersburg PA
CBHW071356280526
45787CB00001B/351